A. Ivanov, Walter E. Gowan

**Russian Grammar**

A. Ivanov, Walter E. Gowan

**Russian Grammar**

ISBN/EAN: 9783743333789

Manufactured in Europe, USA, Canada, Australia, Japa

Cover: Foto ©Paul-Georg Meister /pixelio.de

Manufactured and distributed by brebook publishing software (www.brebook.com)

A. Ivanov, Walter E. Gowan

**Russian Grammar**

# ENGLISH EDITION

OF

## A. IVÁNOFF'S
# RUSSIAN GRAMMAR.

# A. IVÁNOFF'S
# RUSSIAN GRAMMAR

(16th EDITION—145th THOUSAND).

TRANSLATED, ENLARGED, AND ARRANGED

FOR THE

## USE OF ENGLISH STUDENTS OF THE RUSSIAN LANGUAGE

BY

WALTER E. GOWAN,
MAJOR IN HER MAJESTY'S INDIAN ARMY.

LONDON:
KEGAN PAUL, TRENCH & CO., 1, PATERNOSTER SQUARE,
1882.

LONDON:
PRINTED BY GILBERT AND RIVINGTON, LIMITED,
ST. JOHN'S SQUARE, CLERKENWELL.

THE ENGLISH EDITION OF THIS GRAMMAR

IS, BY GRACIOUS PERMISSION,

MOST RESPECTFULLY DEDICATED

TO

HER ROYAL AND IMPERIAL HIGHNESS

MARIE ALEXANDROVNA,

DUCHESS OF EDINBURGH,

AND

IMPERIAL PRINCESS OF RUSSIA.

# TABLE OF CONTENTS (Оглавленіе).

|   | PAGE |
|---|---|
| PREFACE | vii |
| NOTE ON THE RUSSIAN LANGUAGE | ix |
| RUSSIAN, ENGLISH, AND GREEK ALPHABETS | face xi |
| CLASSIFICATION OF RUSSIAN LETTERS | |
| RUSSIAN LETTERS AND THEIR SOUNDS | xi—xx |

*Changes which Russian Letters undergo.*
- PERMUTATION OF RUSSIAN LETTERS . . . . xxi
- EPENTHESIS, OR INSERTION OF LETTERS
- PROSTHESIS, OR PREFIXING OF LETTERS . . . . } xxi & xxii
- APOCOPE, OR ABRIDGMENT OF VOWELS, &c.
- SYNCOPE, OR CONTRACTION OF WORDS BY STRIKING OUT LETTERS

| | |
|---|---|
| CLASSIFICATION OF RUSSIAN WORDS | xxii |
| RUSSIAN WORDS TRACEABLE TO ROOTS | xxii |
| ROOTS OF REGULAR RUSSIAN VERBS | xxiii |
| INTRODUCTION | 1 |
| FIRST PART:— | |
|    ETYMOLOGY | 1—4 |
|    THE NOUN SUBSTANTIVE | 4—26 |
|    THE NOUN ADJECTIVE | 26—39 |
|    THE NOUN OF NUMBER OR NUMERAL | 39—45 |
|    THE PRONOUN | 45—51 |
|    THE VERB | 51—78 |
|    THE ADVERB | 78—81 |
|    THE PREPOSITION | 81, 82 |
|    THE CONJUNCTION | 82, 83 |
|    THE INTERJECTION | 83 |

SECOND PART:—
- SYNTAX
- PROPOSITIONS
- THEIR PRINCIPAL PARTS
- THEIR SECONDARY PARTS
- THE CONSTRUCTION OF A PROPOSITION
- THE SIGNIFICATION OF A PROPOSITION
- THE DIVERSITY OF EXPRESSION IN A PROPOSITION
- CONSTRUCTION OF COMPOUND PROPOSITIONS
- PERIODICAL AND BROKEN SPEECH
- CONCORD OF WORDS
- GOVERNMENT OF WORDS
    - EMPLOYMENT OF CASES WITHOUT PREPOSITIONS
    - EMPLOYMENT OF CASES WITH PREPOSITIONS
- DISTRIBUTION OF WORDS
- MARKS OF PUNCTUATION

THIRD PART:—
- ORTHOGRAPHY
- EMPLOYMENT OF CAPITAL LETTERS
- EMPLOYMENT OF SMALL LETTERS
- PROPER USE OF SEPARATE WORDS
- THE HYPHEN
- DISJOINTING OF WORDS
- CONTRACTION OF WORDS

# PREFACE.

In the belief that, amongst the gradually increasing number of English officers who are recognizing the importance of the study of Russian, a demand exists for a *Modern* Russian Grammar, it occurred to me that I might profitably devote some time and labour, during my leave from India, towards endeavouring to provide for this want.

The method of setting about such a task seemed to me to be one of two :—1st. I might either compile, from the few existing works in the Russian and English languages, a guide of the kind required, and thereby produce that which would of necessity be imperfect, and at the same time far from original. 2nd. Or I might take a practical work, by a recognized Russian Grammarian, and try and adapt it to the special requirements of English Students of the Russian Language.

The latter course I have endeavoured to follow, and the scope of the enlargement and arrangement of the Russian Grammar, which I have selected for the purpose, may be thus explained :—

The original text, having been written by a Russian for Russians contains no Alphabet, or explanations of the various sounds of the several letters. Essentials under this and other heads have been supplied in the first twenty pages of the English edition.

Russian words occurring throughout the English text have been accentuated,[1] so as to ensure, as far as possible, a correct pronunciation.

The final letters or syllables of words, marking the changes to which each is subject either through declension or conjugation, have been printed in a different type, so that the radical letters may stand out more clearly. Prefixes have been similarly dealt with. The principle of reducing every simple and compound word to a root has been thus kept in view.

Mr. Henri Riola, Professor of Russian at the Staff College, has been good enough to help in the revision of the pages of a Grammar which it is hoped will be of use in enabling Englishmen (and especially English officers) to become better acquainted with the language of a great and growing country.

W. E. G.

---

[1] N.B.—Russian words in this Grammar which begin with capital letters, and which are unaccented, take the accent on the initial letter.

# NOTE.

THE Russian language is a dialect of the Slavonian, the common tongue of a large family of nations descended from the Scythians, but whose earlier origin is unascertained. Many of the modern roots are Sanscrit, Greek,[1] Latin, and German. The spoken language incorporated many words from the Polish and other Slavonian dialects, the Tartar and Mongolian. The written character is a very neat one; and the printed has much resemblance to the Greek, some also to the Latin. The Alphabet is as nearly phonetic as can be desired, and has the advantage of expressing complex consonantal sounds. That Russian literature has not yet contributed its full quota to the great hive of human learning should be mainly ascribed to over-government, to its being yet in the youth of its existence, and still in a condition which compels it to borrow much. When civilization shall have taken firm root in all classes, then Russia will no doubt enlarge her pretensions; but the time is coming, and the minds to do the work are ripening.—*Extract from the " Encyclopædia Britannica."*

[1] In the 9th century, two Greek Missionaries were sent into Moravia by the Byzantian Emperor, Michael III., to translate the Bible, and other theological works, into Slavonian. Finding letters unknown to the inhabitants, they composed an Alphabet after the model of the Greek, with a few additional characters, to express the sounds peculiar to the Slavonian langunge.—*Extract from the Introduction to " Heard's Practical Grammar o the Russian Language."* St. Petersburg, 1827.

# RUSSIAN LETTERS AND THEIR SOUNDS.

## Vowels[1] and Semi-Vowels.

(1) The hard vowel А, а, is represented by

| English letters. | English words. |
|---|---|
| á | are, far. |
| ă | am, fat. |
| ō | own, alone. |
| ā | fate. |

The ordinary sound of the Russian а is that of á: *Ex.* мать, mother, pronounced mát'.

It has also the sound of ă when found at the end of certain words and *not accented*: *Ex.* бáба, old woman, pronounced bábă.

In the inflection аго of adjectives, if it be *accented*, its sound is that of ō: *Ex.* сухáго, gen. of сухóй, dry, pronounced sookhōvă.

Note.—When it is *unaccented*, and follows certain consonants (ж, ч, ш, щ), its sound is that of ā: *Ex.* жарá, heat; часы́, hours; шалýнъ, a wag; щажý, I spare, from щадить; pronounced jārá, tchāsoui, shālōōn, shtshājōō.

(2) The soft vowel Я, я, is represented by

| English letters. | English words. |
|---|---|
| yá or yă | yard, yarrow. |
| yĕ | yes. |
| ā | made. |
| á | solar. |

When it is *accented*, and in any part of a word or syllable, its sound is that of yá: *Ex.* я́ма, ditch; мя́со, meat; заря́, dawn: pronounced yámă, myásŏ, zaryá.

When *not accented*, and at the end of words, its sound is that of yă: *Ex.* вре́мя, time, pronounced vrēmyă.

[1] In the pronunciation of Russian vowels it should be noticed whether the word in which they occur is isolated, whether the vowel itself is accented, and whether it begins a syllable.

When *not accented*, and at the beginning of words or syllables, its sound is that of *yĕ*: *Ex.* ядро́, kernel; де́вять, nine : pronounced *yĕdrō*, *devyĕt'*.

After a consonant, and *not accented*, it has the sound of *ā*: *Ex.* вяжу́, I tie (from вяза́ть), pronounced *vājoó*.

The letter я, in the suffix ся, of pronominal and other verbs, is pronounced *sa*: *Ex.* стара́ться, to endeavour; represented thus— *starátsa*.

|  | English letter. | English words. |
|---|---|---|
| (3) The hard vowel Э, э, is represented by | e | enmity, let. |

This letter, and *not e*, is used at the beginning of certain Russian words, and of foreign words in use in the Russian language, and also after a vowel: *Ex.* эй! ho! охъ! hey! э́тотъ, this, &c.; эква́торъ, the Equator; поэ́тъ, poet; pronounced *eĭ*, *ekh*, *etot*, *ekvátor*, *poet*.

|  | English letters. | English words. |
|---|---|---|
| (4) The soft vowel E, e, is represented by | yĕ | yes. |
|  | yō | yoke. |
|  | yŏ | yonder. |
|  | ŏ | sop. |
|  | ĭ | sit. |
|  | ĕ | spell. |

At the commencement of words or syllables, and after a vowel, its sound is that of *yĕ*: *Ex.* едва́, scarcely; вели́кое, great (*neut. form* of вели́кій): pronounced *yĕdvá* and *vĕlēēkōyĕ*.

When it is *accented* it takes the sound of *yō* or *yŏ*: *Ex.* ёлка, a fir-tree; твёрдо, firmly; pronounced *yōlkă* and *tvyŏrdă*.

In such cases in this Grammar it will be found marked with two dots instead of the ordinary accent mark.

When *accented*, and found after the consonants ж, ч, ш, щ and ц, it has the sound of *ŏ*: *Ex.* жёлчь, gall, pronounced *jŏltch'*, and marked as above indicated.

After a consonant, when *not accented*, its sound is that of *ĭ*: *Ex.* жена́, wife, pronounced *jĭná*.

After a consonant (other than those specified above), when *accented*, its sound is that of *ĕ*: *Ex.* смерть, death; се́рдце, heart; pronounced *smĕrt'* and *sĕrdtse*.

Note.—The vowel *e* is used, instead of *э*, in the following Russian words:—прое́ктъ, project; рее́стръ, register; ефе́съ, sword-hilt; ефре́йторъ, a corporal, &c.; which are pronounced proékt, reestr, efes, efreitor, &c.

(5) The hard vowel *Ы, ы,* has no *exact* equivalent in English. It has a hollow or muffled sound, and its true pronunciation can only be seized by hearing it from the mouth of a Russian.

After the letters *б, в, м, п, ф,* its sound resembles the French *oui* pronounced very shortly, or that of the English *we* : *Ex.* грибы́ (*plur.* of грпбъ, a mushroom) : вы, you ; мы, we ; снопы́ (*plur.* of снопъ, a sheaf) : pronounced grib*oui,* v*oui,* m*oui,* snăp*oui,* &c.

After other consonants its sound is that of the English *uee* : *Ex.* сынъ, a son, pronounced s*ueen.*

Note.—This vowel may always be distinguished from *u* by its thicker sound. It occurs in the genitive case singular, and nominative case plural, of substantives ending in *a,* and in the nominative, plural, of those ending in *ъ.*

|  | English letters. | English words. |
|---|---|---|
| (6) The soft vowel *u* is represented by the | ĭ | ill. |
|  | æ | æra. |
|  | ye |  |
|  | oui |  |

Its ordinary sound at the commencement of words and syllables is that of *i* : *Ex.* идти́, to go ; pronounced *i*dteē : and also in the word миръ, peace, pronounced mĭr.

At the commencement of certain cases of the pronoun of the third person it bears the sound of a diphthong : *Ex.* ихъ, of them, theirs, pronounced *æ*kh.

After the semi-vowel *ь,* it has the sound of *ye* : *Ex.* статьи́ (*plur.* of статья́, an article), pronounced staty*é*.

Note 1.—After a preposition ending in *ъ,* it takes the thicker sound of *ы* : *Ex.* предъиду́щій, preceding, pronounced pred*oui*-dooshtshiĭ, &c. Indeed, some writers substitute the letter *ы* for the combined letters *ъи* shown in the above example.

Note 2.—Many writers retain *u* in all words composed of the preposition *при* and a word commencing with a vowel : *Ex.* приобща́ть, to communicate ; прие́хать, to arrive, &c. But it is more regular to change the *u* into *i,* and to write such words thus : пріобща́ть and пріе́хать, &c.

(7) The soft vowel *I, i*, is represented by the

| English letter. | English words. |
|---|---|
| ĭ | pity. ill. |

Its ordinary sound is that of the English *i*: *Ex.* лилія, lily, pronounced leēlĭyă.

Before a consonant this vowel is only met with in one word in the whole of the Russian language, viz. мíръ, universe, pronounced mĭr, and which should not be confounded with the word миръ, peace (see second illustration of the *ordinary* sound of *и*).

NOTE 1.—The vowel *i* is used instead of *и*, of which it is, indeed, a shorter form, before all vowels and before the semi-vowel *й*: *Ex.* сіé (*neut.* form of сей, this or that): пріучáть, to accustom; пріятный, agreeable; гéній, genius, &c.

NOTE 2.—The letters *и* and *i* are exactly similar in sound; the first is used before consonants, and the second before vowels: *Ex.* долúна, a valley; Іюль, July; мѣльница, a mill; чтéніе, reading; вúшня, a cherry; насúліе, violence.

(8) The hard vowel *O, o*, is represented by

| English letters. | English words. |
|---|---|
| ō | no. |
| ŏ | not. |
| ă | was. |

The ordinary sound of this letter is that of the English *ō* or *ŏ*: *Ex.* дóма, of a house, or the idiom for "at home;" кóлоколъ, a bell: pronounced dōmă and kōlŏkŏl.

When, however, it occurs in a syllable upon which the accent does *not* fall, its pronunciation is that of the English *ă*: *Ex.* хорошó, well, pronounced khărăshō.

(9) The hard vowel *Y, y*, is represented by

| English letters. | English word. |
|---|---|
| oo | moon. |

The sound of this letter resembles that of the English *ōō* or *ŏŏ*: *Ex.* бýря, tempest; губá, creek, bay; pronounced bōōryă and gŏŏbá.

(10) The soft vowel *Ю, ю*, is represented by

| English letters. | English words. |
|---|---|
| yu | you. |
| u | tube. |

At the beginning of words or syllables the sound of this letter is that of the English *yū*: *Ex.* югъ, south, pronounced yūg.

( xv )

At the end, or in the middle, of words or syllables, its sound is that of the English *u* : *Ex*. люблю́, I love, pronounced l*ŭ*bl*ŭ*.

(11) The medium vowel Ѣ, ѣ, has for the most part the same sounds as the Russian E, e (see above, letter No. 4), viz. that of the following English letters : *yĕ* in the word *yes*, and of *yo* or *yeo* in the words *yoke* or *yonder* and *yeoman*, and also that of *ay* in the word *may*.

At the commencement, and sometimes in the middle, of words and syllables, its sound is that of *ye* : *Ex*. ѣсть, to eat ; нѣтъ, no, not ; pronounced y*ĕ*st' and ny*ĕ*tt.

When *accented* it has the sound of *yeo* only in the words звѣ́зды (*plur.* of звѣзда́, a star) ; гнѣ́зда (*plur.* of гнѣздо́, a nest) ; сѣ́дла (*plur.* of сѣдло́, a saddle), &c., and their derivatives ; pronounced zv*yeŏ*zdwi, g*n͞yeŏ*zd*ă*, sy*eŏ*dl*ă*. Also цвѣ́лъ, past tense of цвѣсти́, to blossom ; обрѣ́лъ, past tense of обрѣсти́, to acquire ; pronounced tsv*yeŏ*l and ăbr*yeŏ*l, &c.

When *accented* and at the end, and sometimes in the middle, of a word or syllable, its sound is that of *ay* : *Ex*. на столѣ́, on the table (from столъ) ; вѣ́ра, faith ; pronounced ná stol*áy* and v*áy*r*ă*.

NOTE.—As a general rule, it may be observed that when a primitive word or root is written with ѣ, that vowel is retained in all its derivatives.

(12, 13, 14) The semi-vowels ъ, ь, й, have no separate sounds of their own.

Since no Russian word can end with a consonant, the hard or soft semi-vowel, ъ or ь, forms the termination of such as do not end with a vowel : *Ex*. глаго́лъ, a verb ; вѣтвь, a branch, &c.

The hard semi-vowel ъ, though mute, gives to the *consonant* which precedes it a strong and dry sound, as though it were double. It causes, too, a feeble consonant to be articulated like its corresponding strong consonant : *Ex*. станъ, stage, station ; вязъ, elm ; кровъ, roof ; шестъ, pole, perch ; братъ, brother, &c. ; pronounced stá*nn*, vya*ss*, kro*ff*, shes*tt*, brâ*tt*.

In the prefixes, into the composition of which the hard semi-vowel ъ enters, it is only retained before the vowels *е, и, ѣ, ю, я* : *Ex*. объекти́вный, objective ; въѣ́хать, to enter ; предъиду́щій, preceding ; адъюта́нтъ, aide-de-camp ; объяви́ть, to announce, &c.

The soft semi-vowel ь may be said to be a modified form of *u*. It gives to the *consonant* which precedes it a soft and liquid sound : *Ex*. станъ, arise (imp. mood of станови́ться) ; вязь, swamp, band ;

кровь, blood; шесть, six; брать, to take; pronounced stan$^y$, vyaz$^y$, krov$^y$, shest$^y$, brá$^y$, leaving the original sound of the final *u* to melt away in the mouth. In the middle of a word or syllable the same process takes place.

NOTE 1.—The semi-vowel ь cannot be placed either after the guttural letters г, к, х, or the liquid ц. It may appear, however, after any of the other consonants, and that, too, in the middle of a word: *Ex.* весьма́, very; ско́лько, how much, how many, &c.

NOTE 2.—When the letter л occurs before the termination *путь*, the soft semi-vowel ь is inserted: *Ex.* коло́ть, to pierce, колъпу́ть; стрѣля́ть, to fire, стрѣлъпу́ть, &c.

NOTE 3.—The importance of distinguishing between the hard and soft semi-vowels ъ and ь will be seen by a reference to the following words, the signification of which depends on the pronunciation of the final consonant:—

| | |
|---|---|
| братъ, brother; | брать, to take. |
| вязъ, an elm; | вязь, a bog, band. |
| кладъ, a treasure; | кладь, cargo. |
| кровъ, a roof; | кровь, blood. |
| матъ, mate (at chess); | мать, mother. |
| перстъ, a finger; | персть, earth. |
| плотъ, a raft; | плоть, flesh. |
| пылъ, heat; | пыль, dust. |
| столъ, a table; | столь, so much. |
| у́голъ, a corner; | у́голь, coal (charcoal). |
| цѣпъ, a flail; | цѣпь, a chain. |
| шестъ, a pole; | шесть, six. |
| щегóлъ, a goldfinch; | щёголь, a fop. |

&c., &c.

The soft semi-vowel *й* is always found after a vowel, and is but a shortened form of *и*. Its pronunciation is very brief, and, in conjunction with the vowel which precedes it, it forms but one syllable: *Ex.* дай, give (imp. mood of дава́ть); мой, my, mine; pronounced dá$^y$, mō$^y$, &c.

## CONSONANTS.[1]

(15) The labial and strong consonant П, п, is in sound similar to the English *p*: *Ex.* попъ, a priest, pronounced *pope*.

---

[1] In the pronunciation of Russian consonants, it should be observed whether the following vowel is hard or soft, and whether such vowel terminates the word or syllable.

( xvii )

(16) The ordinary sound of the feeble consonant Б, б, is that of the English b.

It moreover takes the sound of its corresponding strong consonant п at the end of words or syllables terminating with the hard semi-vowel ъ and before any strong consonant: *Ex.* бобъ bean; обтирать, to rub round; pronounced bo*pp* and ă*p*tirát'.

(17) The sound of the labial and strong consonant ф is that of the English *f* or *ph*: *Ex.* франтъ, a beau or fop, pronounced *f*rant.

(18) The ordinary sound of the labial and feeble consonant В, в, is that of the English *v*: *Ex.* вѣра, faith, pronounced *v*āyra.

It, moreover, takes the sound of its corresponding strong consonant ф at the end of words or syllables terminating with the hard semi-vowel ъ and before any strong consonant: *Ex.* ровъ, ditch; вшóрникъ, Tuesday; pronounced ro*ff* and *f*tórnik.

(19) The ordinary sound of the guttural and strong consonant К, к, is that of the English *k* and of *c* in certain examples.

Moreover, before the feeble consonants б, д, ж, з, it takes the sound of its corresponding feeble consonant *г*: *Ex.* къ Бóгу, to God; къ добру́, to the good; къ землѣ, towards the earth; pronounced *g*bōhŏŏ, *g*dăbrōō, *g*zemlāy, &c.

Before the strong consonants к, т, ч, it receives the aspirated articulation of *x*: *Ex.* къ комý? towards whom? кто? who? къ чемý? towards whom?—pronounced '*k*omōō, '*k*to, '*k*tchemōō, &c.

(20) At the beginning, and in the middle, of certain words the guttural and feeble consonant Г, г, preserves the sound of the English *g*: *Ex.* гром̃ъ, thunder; гербъ, coat of arms; тйбну, I will perish; pronounced *g*rom, *g*erb, *g*ēēbnŏŏ.

It has also other sounds. At the end of words and before the consonant ш it takes the sound of its corresponding strong consonant к: *Ex.* могъ, I could (from мочь), pronounced mō*k*.

It is aspirated in the following words: Бóга, of God; Госпóдь, Lord; блáго, good, well; pronounced Bó*h*ă, *H*ăspōd', blá*h*o.

In the words Богъ, God, убóгъ (it is) wretched; also before a strong consonant (к, т, ч, &c.), and in foreign words ending in ргъ, such as Страсбýргъ, Strasbo*urg*, it takes the aspirated sound of the strong consonant х, which may be represented by *kh*. Hence the above words are pronounced Bo*kh*, ŏŏbo*kh*, Strasbour*kh*.

In the terminations аго, яго, ого and его of adjectives and of

*b*

pronouns, its sound is that of the English *v* : *Ex.* красна*го*, of red; си́ня*го*, of blue; одно*го́*, of one; все*го́*, of all; pronounced krásnăvă, sēēnyăvă, ădnăvō, vsevō.

In foreign words adopted in the Russian language it is pronounced either as the English *g* or *h*, according to the sound of the letter which it replaces : *Ex.* *г*ра́ція, grace; *г*о́спиталь, hospital; pronounced *g*rátsĭyă, *h*ospĭtál'.

(21) The sound of the guttural and strong consonant *X, x*, is that of *kh* :[1] *Ex.* *х*рамъ, temple, church; pronounced *kh*ramm.

(22) The ordinary sound of the dental and strong consonant *T, m*, is that of the English *t* : *Ex.* *т*еле́га, a cart or waggon, pronounced *t*elāyga.

Before the feeble consonants б, г, д, ж, з, this letter takes the sound of its corresponding feeble consonant д : *Ex.* о́*т*далъ, I have surrendered; о́*т*зывъ, recall; pronounced ō*dd*al; ō*d*zwiff.

In words wherein *cm* is followed by *н*, the letter *m* is not pronounced : *Ex.* по́*ст*ный, abstinent; ча́*ст*ный, private; pronounced pōsnwĭĭ, tchásnwĭĭ.

(23) The ordinary sound of the dental and feeble consonant Д, д, is that of the English *d* : *Ex.* *д*омъ, a house, pronounced *d*om.

This letter, moreover, takes the sound of its corresponding strong consonant *m* at the end of words and syllables terminating with the hard semi-vowel ъ, and when found before any strong consonant : *Ex.* са*д*ъ, garden; во́*д*ка, brandy or whiskey; pronounced sá*tt*, vō*t*ka.

In words wherein *зд* is followed by *н*, the letter *д* is not pronounced : *Ex.* по́*зд*но, late, (*adv.*) пра́*зд*никъ, holiday; pronounced pōznă, práznik.

(24) The buzzing or hissing and strong consonant Ш, *ш*, resembles in sound the compound English letter *sh* : *Ex.* *ш*кафъ, cupboard, pronounced *sh*kaff.

(25) The ordinary sound of the buzzing or hissing and feeble consonant Ж, *ж*, is that of the compound English letter *zh*, or the French *j* : *Ex.* *ж*ду, I wait (from *ж*дать); му*ж*ъ, husband; ло́*ж*а, butt; pronounced *zh*doo, moo*j*, lō*j*kă.

This letter, however, takes the sound of its corresponding strong

---

[1] There are no *English* words that properly exemplify the very guttural sound of the Russian *х*, but the sound of *ch* in the *Scotch* word *loch* is very like it.

consonant ш at the end of words and syllables terminating with the hard semi-vowel ъ, and when found before any strong consonant: *Ex.* ножъ, knife; кружка, tankard, jug; pronounced nō*sh*, kroō*shk*ă.

(26) The ordinary sound of the hissing and strong consonant С, с, is that of the English *s*: *Ex.* сестра́, sister, pronounced *s*estrá.

Before the feeble consonants б, *i*, д, ж, з, this letter takes the sound of its corresponding feeble consonant з: *Ex.* сборъ, collection; сгорѣть, to burn; сдать, to surrender; сжимать, to compress; pronounced *z*bor, *z*gorătʸ, *z*dátʸ, *z*jĭmátʸ.

Before ш and ч this letter takes the hissing sound of ш: *Ex.* сшивать, to sew together; счастіе, prosperity; pronounced *shsh*ĭvátʸ, *shch*ástĭye.

(27) The ordinary sound of the hissing and feeble consonant З, з, is that of the English *z*: *Ex.* звонъ, ringing (sound), pronounced *z*von.

This letter also takes the sound of its corresponding strong consonant с at the end of words or syllables terminating with the hard semi-vowel ъ, and when it is found before any strong consonant: *Ex.* возъ, a load; сказка, tale, fable; pronounced vo*ss*; ská*s*kă.

NOTE.—The з of the particles из, воз, раз, is changed into с when the word with which they are to be connected begins with a hard consonant:—

    *Ex.* из . . . истребить, to destroy.
         воз . . . воскресеніе, resurrection.
         раз . . . распечатать, to unseal.

(28) The sound of the lingual and strong consonant Ц, ц, is that of the compound English letter *ts*: *Ex.* царь, Tsar or Russian Emperor's title; перецъ, pepper; pronounced *ts*árʸ, pĕrĕ*ts*.

(29) The sound of the buzzing or hissing and strong consonant Ч, ч, is that of the compound English letters *ch* or *tch*: *Ex.* чепчикъ, cap or cowl, pronounced *tch*ĕp*tch*ĭk.

In the word что, what that, (pronounced *sh*tō), and before the consonant н, the same letter takes the sound of ш: *Ex.* нарочно, designedly, pronounced nărō*sh*nă.

The word точно exactly, is, however, pronounced to*tch*nă, to distinguish it from тошно, to have nausea, pronounced tŏ*sh*nă.

(30) The sound of the buzzing or hissing and strong consonant

Щ, щ, is that of the compound English letters *shch* or *shtsh*: *Ex.* щитъ, shield, pronounced *shtsheet*ʸ.

Before the consonant *n* the same letter has the simple sound of *ш*: *Ex.* помо́щникъ, assistant, pronounced pămŏ*sh*nĭk.

(31) The sound of the palatal and liquid consonant Л, л, is *approximately* that of the English *l*: *Ex.* долъ, dale, valley; боль, pain; pronounced do*l*, bo*l*ʸ.

(32) The sound of the labial and liquid consonant M, м, is that of the English letter *m*: *Ex.* мать, mother, pronounced *m*átʸ.

(33) The sound of the palatal and liquid consonant Н, н, is that of the English *n*: *Ex.* нашъ, our, ours; онъ, he; pronounced *n*ásh, ŏ*n*.

(34) The sound of the palatal and liquid consonant P, p, is that of the English *r broadly articulated*: *Ex.* родъ, gender, race; pronounced *r*ōd.

N.B.—The letters ѵ, ѳ, have been omitted from these observations, because the first is practically obsolete, whilst the use of the second is confined to a few words only, taken from the Greek, in which its sound may be represented by the English letters *th*. Explanation, moreover, of the sounds of the letter *r* will be found in § 8, page 2, of the Grammar.

Although an endeavour has been made to explain the pronunciation of the Russian letters, it must be confessed that all attempts to express the sounds of one language by the characters of another are imperfect, *oral* instruction being the only sure means of acquiring a correct pronunciation.

## CHANGES WHICH RUSSIAN LETTERS UNDERGO.

Most of the apparent irregularities of Russian Etymology being founded upon the mutability of the letters, the Student is advised to pay particular attention to that part of the Grammar which treats of their changes and reciprocal effect upon each other in the formation of derivatives, and in the declension and modification of words. These changes will explain the omission of some rules that are to be found in other Grammars, but which are rendered superfluous by a knowledge of the more fundamental rules relating to the letters.

# PERMUTATION OF RUSSIAN VOWELS, SEMI-VOWELS, AND CONSONANTS, SUBJECT TO THE VARIOUS RULES OF DERIVATION, DECLENSION, AND CONJUGATION.

## Vowels and Semi-Vowels.

| | | | | |
|---|---|---|---|---|
| 1. и | | i | | *any* other vowel. |
| 2. ъ | | о | before | *any two* consonants. |
| 3. ь and й | | е | | *any* consonant. |
| 4. я | | а | | |
| 5. ю | change into | у | | г, к, х, ж, ч, ш, щ, ц. |
| 6. ы | | п | | г, к, х, ж, ч, ш, щ. |
| 7. е | | о | after | г, к, х. |
| 8. о | | е | | ж, ч, ш, щ, ц. |
| 9. ѣ | | и | | ´i. |
| 10. ь | | й | | *any vowel.* |

## Consonants.

| | | | | |
|---|---|---|---|---|
| 11. г | | | | и, у, ь. |
| 12. д | | ж | | я, е, и, у, ю, ь. |
| 13. з | | | | |
| 14. к | | | | и, ю, ь. |
| 15. т | change into | ч | before | я, е, и, у, ю, ь. |
| 16. ц | | | | е, и, у, ь. |
| 17. х | | ш | | и, у, ь. |
| 18. с | | | | |
| 19. ск | | щ | | я, е, и, у, ю, ь. |
| 20. ст | | | | |

## Epenthesis.

*Epenthesis,* or the insertion of a letter in the middle of a word, is exemplified as follows: (*a*) the vowels *o* and *e* are inserted between two consonants at the end of words: *Ex.* ого́нь, fire; вѣтеръ, wind;— (*b*) the consonant *л* is inserted after the letters *б, в, м, п, ф,* when they would otherwise be followed by *ю* or *е*: *Ex.* люблю́, I love (from люби́ть); деше́вле, cheaper (from де́шево), &c.;—(*c*) the consonant *н* is prefixed to the pronoun of the third person when it stands after a preposition or an adverb: *Ex.* у него́, he had; про́тивъ нихъ, against them.

## PROSTHESIS.

*Prosthesis* is the placing of a letter at the beginning of a word to facilitate pronunciation: *Ex.* вóсемь, eight, instead of óсемь; оржанóй, of rye, instead of ржанóй.

## APOCOPE.

*Apocope* is the modifying of a vowel at the end of a word: *Ex.* чтобъ, in order that, instead of чтобы; со мной, with me, instead of со мнóю, &c.

## SYNCOPE.

*Syncope* is the striking out of a letter from the middle of a word to facilitate or soften the pronunciation: *Ex.* полторá, 1½, instead of полеторá, &c.

## CLASSIFICATION OF RUSSIAN WORDS.

All Russian words are either *primitive* (первообрáзное)—*Ex.* садъ, garden; or *derivative* (произвóдное)—*Ex.* садóвникъ, garden*er*; or *compound* (слóжное)—*Ex.* садовóдство, garden*ing* (from садъ, garden, and водúть, to conduct).

## RUSSIAN WORDS TRACEABLE TO ROOTS.

Every Russian word is, moreover, traceable to a *root* (кóрень), or reducible to certain *radical* syllables or letters which become words by the junction of other syllables or letters. Roots may be divided into *principal* and *secondary*. From the *principal* (глáвный) roots denominative words or parts of speech can be formed by the mere addition of a semi-vowel or a vowel: *Ex.* from the root *вид* comes видъ, sight; from the root *рук* comes рукá, a hand. The *secondary* (придáточный) roots are subdivided into, (*a*) *initial* (предъидýщій), which consist of auxiliary words or particles in union with other principal roots at the beginning of which they are placed. These are called *prefixes* or *prepositions*: *Ex.* у-хóдъ, departure; от-кáзъ, refusal, &c.;—(*b*) *final* (послѣдующій), or such as form the termination of other principal roots. These are called *suffixes*: *Ex.* вод-á, water, дѣл-*атъ*, to do, &c.

The roots of the following words can at once be traced after removing their prefixes and affixes, and then reducing compound words to derivative, and derivative to primitive, as seen above :—

преизбы́точествовать, to superabound (root *быт*).
засвидѣтельствованіе, attestation (root *вид*).
независимость, independence (root *вис*).
неизмѣри́мый, immeasurable (root *мѣр*).
предсѣда́тельствовать, to preside (root *сѣд*).
сострада́ніе, compassion (root *страд*).
изобрѣта́тельность, inventive faculty (root *брѣт*).
вспомога́тельный, auxiliary (root *мог*).
удовлетвори́тельный, satisfactory (root *твор*), &c.

## ROOTS OF REGULAR RUSSIAN VERBS.

The root of regular Russian verbs can be ascertained by striking off the final letters *ть* of the infinite mood of the imperfect aspect, together with any of the preceding vowels *а, и, ѣ, о, у, е, я*.

# ERRATA.

| Page | Line | For | Read | Page | Line | For | Read |
|---|---|---|---|---|---|---|---|
| 2 | 25 | лёгкій | лёгкій | 54 | 3 | перепдти́ | перейти́ |
| 3 | 33 | паре́чіе | паре́чіе | 55 | 33 | поду́л | поду́л |
| 13 | 23 | ста́росту | ста́рость | 61 | 15 | поиду́ | пойду́ |
| 15 | 5 | зеркал | зеркал | 62 | 18 | раскра́тивать | раскра́шивать |
| „ | 35 | руки́ | ру́ки | 63 | 12 | уви́дал | уви́дал |
| „ | 36 | руки́ | ру́ки | „ | 39 | сту́кну -ншь -нт | сту́кну -ешь -ет |
| 17 | 14 | in the oblique cases | in this one oblique case | | | -имъ -ите -ут | -емъ -ете -ут |
| 18 | 9 | муравёв | муравьёв | 64 | 1 | дѣла́й, живи́ | дѣла́й, живи́ |
| 19 | 18 | пулковъ | чулковъ | „ | 45 | ви́дывавшій | ви́дывавшій |
| 20 | 18 | on | in | 65 | 5 | сдѣ́лавъ | сдѣ́лавъ |
| „ | 20 | медвѣпёпокъ | медвѣжёнокъ | 67 | 42 | praising himself | praising one's self |
| „ | 22 | львёнки and мышёнки | львёнки and мышёнки | 68 | 3 | улыбну́вшись | улыба́вшись |
| | | | | 69 | 44 | o | or |
| | | | | 71 | 5 | ѣзшать | ѣзжа́ть |
| „ | „ | льва́та | льва́та | 72 | 18 | prefixes | aspects |
| 21 | 2 | церкви́ | це́ркви | 74 | 31 | work | wink |
| „ | 8 | „ | „ | 76 | 16 | смотря́шійся | смотря́щійся |
| „ | 27 | воробьёй | воробёй | „ | 22 | ый, ая, ее | ый, ая, ое |
| 22 | 4 | коте́л | коте́л | „ | 37 | by means of either | from either |
| „ | 5 | note | knot | | | | |
| „ | 17 | Ви́хор, ви́хра | Ви́хор, вихра́ | 78 | 9 | force | voice |
| 24 | 21 | пе́тля | петля́ | „ | 24 | пюсколько | нѣсколько |
| 27 | 3 | сего́дняшный | сего́дняшній | „ | 27 | весьта́ | весьма́ |
| „ | 14 | усѣ́ченный | усѣ́ченный | 79 | 1 | провожда́ть | проводи́ть |
| „ | 18 | вели́к -а́ -о | вели́к -а́ -ó | 80 | 6 | не по, нѣт not | не не, нѣт no |
| 28 | 16 | чёрныя | чёрный | „ | 15 | таки́м | таки́м |
| 29 | 22 | най. найлу́чшій | най, найлу́чшій | 82 | 18 | вѣд | вѣдь |
| „ | 23 | наибо́лѣе | наибо́лѣе | 84 | 28 | adjective про́-шлый | past tense of пройти́ |
| 30 | 6 | ни́же | ни́же | | | | |
| „ | 7 | найлу́чшій | найлу́чшій | 88 | 10 | not so | not to |
| „ | 8 | найху́дшій | найху́дшій | „ | 35 | пе́рвым | пе́рвым |
| 33 | 19 | сёстер | сестёр | 90 | 18 | и | я |
| „ | 23 | „ | „ | „ | 28 | возовпови́лись | возобнови́лись |
| 36 | 7 | оле́ньяго | оле́ньей | 91 | 6 | Kalmucks, a | Kalmucks are a |
| „ | 8 | оле́ньему | „ | „ | 23 | изоби́лій | изоби́лія |
| 39 | 28 | два, sing., for all genders | два, sing., for masc. & neut. | 92 | 14 | Россі́й | Россі́и |
| | | | | „ | 20 | мольбы́ | мольбы́ |
| „ | 29 | двѣ, plur. | двѣ, fem. | 93 | 2 | сраже́ній | сраже́нія |
| 41 | 2 | полови́на | полови́на | „ | 8 | мно́жество | мно́жество |
| 46 | 6 | собо́ю | собо́ю | 94 | 8 | чье | чьё |
| „ | 12 | -ые -ыя | -іе -ія | „ | 24 | минера́льных | минера́льных |
| 47 | 11 | „ „ | „ „ | 95 | 14 | сочине́ніи | сочине́ній |
| „ | 14 | „ „ | „ „ | „ | 34 | требова́ть | требова́ть |
| 50 | 8 | бпхыъ | бныхъ | 97 | 2 | войска | войска́ |
| 52 | 3 | что ! | (что) ? | „ | 13 | жертвова́ть | жертвова́ть |
| „ | 25 | щебече́т, ржст | щебече́т, ржёт | „ | 18 | завѣ́дываніе | завѣ́дываніе |
| „ | 27 | воетъ | вóет | 98 | 25 | ми́лосты | ми́лости |
| „ | 28 | мыча́тъ | мыча́т | 99 | 29 | морем | мо́рем |
| „ | 29 | блеет | блеет | 105 | 34 | А́лпы | А́льпы |
| „ | 30 | мяукает | мяу́кает | „ | 37 | Алпійских | Альпі́йских |
| „ | „ | свинья́ | свинья́ | 107 | 28 | Со́лнце | Со́лнце |
| „ | 31 | хрюкает | хрю́кает | 109 | 23 | короле́вское | Короле́вское |
| „ | „ | воркует | ворку́ет | 110 | 18 | Институ́т | Институ́т |
| „ | 32 | клокчет | клóхчет | „ | 26 | Рождество́ | Рождество́ |
| „ | 33 | квакает | ква́кает | „ | 28 | подвя́зки | Подвя́зки |
| „ | 34 | жужжат | жужжа́т | 111 | 8 | проншше́ствіе | происше́ствіе |
| „ | 35 | жужжа́т | жужжа́ть | 112 | 9 | вѣде́ніе | вѣде́ніе |
| 53 | 30 | скри́пкѣ | скри́пкѣ | „ | 67 | желѣза | желѣза́ |

# INTRODUCTION.

§ 1. Russian Grammar elucidates those rules of the Russian language which should be adhered to, both in Conversation and in Writing.

§ 2. In order to correctly express our thoughts, we must know, (1) the proper use and meaning of words in all their inflections or changes; (2) how to connect such words so that the sense of our expressions may be perfectly clear; (3) how to write words in conformity with rules laid down by the best authors.

§ 3. Agreeably to the above requirements, Grammar divides itself into three parts:—

    I.   *Etymology*   (Словопроизведéніе).
   II.  *Syntax*   (Словосочинéніе).
  III.  *Orthography*  (Правописáніе).

# FIRST PART.

### ETYMOLOGY.

§ 4. Under the head of Etymology are explained, (1) the *derivation* (происхождéніе), (2) the *construction* (состáвъ), (3) the *signification* (значéніе), and (4) the *changes* (перемѣна [1]) of words.

§ 5. A word may express any sort of idea or feeling: *Ex.* другъ friend, мóре sea, скрóмность modesty, дóбрый good, kind, пять five,

---

[1] All Russian words placed within brackets after English words are in their primary terminations. They are so placed in order to let the student see, without search, what are the corresponding Russian equivalents for such terms as are in common use in every grammar. *Trans.*

Я I, уважа́ть to consider, читáющій[1] he who reads, бѣ́гая[2] running, зáвтра to-morrow, мéжду amongst, between, слѣ́довательно consequently, ахъ! ah! oh! Ой oh! ah!

§ 6. Words are made up of *syllables* (слогъ), and syllables of *letters* (бу́ква).

§ 7. A letter is that which is produced by separate sounds of the voice.

§ 8. There are thirty-six letters in the Russian Alphabet.[3]

    *Obs.*—The Slavonic letter ѵ is pronounced in a twofold manner, (1) as *u* in the word му́ро chrism or holy oil, and сѵно́дъ synod; and (2) as *в* in the words Еванге́ліе Gospel, and Иса́ѵъ Esau. The letter ѵ is only used in modern Russian in the word му́ро, and its derivatives, such as муропома́заніе rite of anointing, муропо́сица bearer of the holy oil, etc.

§ 9. Russian letters are divided into *vowels* (гла́сная бу́ква), *semi-vowels* (полугла́сная бу́ква), and *consonants* (согла́сная бу́ква).

§ 10. The vowels are pronounced without the aid of other letters. They are as follows :—а, е, и, і, о, у, ы, ѣ, э, ю, я.

    *N.B.*—The vowel е accented is pronounced in several words like іо (йо): *Ex.* ёлка fir-tree, лёдъ ice, мёдъ honey, mead, поётъ[4] he, she, or it sings. In such cases two dots are sometimes placed over the letter е, thus ё.

§ 11. The semi-vowel й (or *и* short) is written and *pronounced* after *vowels*: *Ex.* Андре́й Andrew, лёгкій light, поко́йный tranquil. The semi-vowels ъ and ь are employed after consonants. Ъ gives them a hard sound: *Ex.* столъ table, отъѣ́здъ departure. But ь gives a soft sound to the consonant which precedes it: *Ex.* сто́ль so much, so many, дѣ́льный business-like.

    The letter ѵ (и́жица, name of this Slavonic letter), as has been said in the observation at foot of § 8, is pronounced in a twofold way, viz. either like the vowel *u*, or like the

---

[1] First person, singular number, present participle, active, of the verb читáть, to read. *Trans.*

[2] Present gerund of the verb бѣ́гать, to run. *Trans.*

[3] See Table facing p. xi. *Trans.*

[4] Third person, singular number, present tense, of the verb пѣть, to sing. *Trans.*

consonant в. In the first case, therefore, it may be reckoned as a vowel, and in the second as a consonant.

§ 12. The consonants are uttered with the aid of vowels. The consonants are б, в, г, д, ж, з, к, л, м, н, п, р, с, т, ф, х, ц, ч, ш, щ, ѳ.

§ 13. One vowel, or the coupling of one or more vowels with semi-vowels or consonants, forms a syllable: *Ex.* а, о, у, я, изъ, отъ, ай, ей, при-стро́-ить, от-дѣ́ль-ный, у-кра-шé-ні-е.

§ 14. Words are made up of one or more syllables, and are classified as *mono-syllabic* (односло́жное), *dis-syllabic* (двусло́жное), *tri-syllabic* (трехсло́жное), and *poly-syllabic* (многосло́жное): *Ex.* полкъ regiment, за-ко́нъ law, че-ло-вѣ́къ man, со-вер-ше́н-ство perfection.

§ 15. Words may be either *primary* (коренно́е) or *derivative* (производное).

§ 16. Primary words are such as are not derived from other words: *Ex.* весе́лье joy, жалѣть to pity.

§ 17. Derivative words are formed from the primary: *Ex.* весельча́къ merry fellow, весёлый merry, веселиться to make oneself merry, &c., derived from весе́лье; жа́лость pity, сожалѣ́ніе commiseration, жа́лкій miserable, безжа́лостный pitiless, сжа́литься to take pity on, жаль it is a pity, &c., derived from жалѣ́ть.

§ 18. Compound (сло́жное) words are formed by the junction of two or more single words: *Ex.* морепла́ватель navigator, благодѣ́яніе good action, безпристра́стіе impartiality, &c. *Integral* (составно́е) words can be formed in like manner, such as Генера́лъ-Маіо́ръ Major-General, кто-инбу́дь someone, &c.

§ 19. All words in the Russian language are divided, according to their meaning, into nine *parts of speech* (часть рѣ́чи.) These are:—

| | | | |
|---|---|---|---|
| I. | Noun | Substantive | (Имя Существи́тельное). |
| II. | „ | Adjective | (Имя Прилага́тельное). |
| III. | „ | Numeral | (Имя Числи́тельное). |
| IV. | | Pronoun | (Мѣстоимѣ́ніе). |
| V. | | Verb | (Глаго́лъ). |
| VI. | | Adverb | (Нарѣ́чіе). |
| VII. | | Preposition | (Предло́гъ). |
| VIII. | | Conjunction | (Сою́зъ). |
| IX. | | Interjection | (Междоме́тіе). |

§ 20. Words belonging to the first six parts of speech have variable terminations, whereas those belonging to the three last named do not alter in any way.

The Noun Substantive (Имя Существи́тельное).

§ 21. A Noun Substantive is the name of any object: *Ex.* Бо́гъ God, до́мъ house, земля́ earth, терпѣ́ніе patience, ча́съ hour, o'clock, &c.

§ 22. *Objects* (предме́тъ) are (1) *animate* (одушевлённый), *i.e.* those which have life and voluntary motion: *Ex.* человѣ́къ man, Пётръ Peter, &c., &c.

>    *Obs.*—The *names* (и́мя) by which we call people are *personal* (ли́чный) objects: *Ex.* бра́тъ brother, сестра́ sister, Алекса́ндръ, Alexander, Ма́рья Mary, полко́вникъ colonel, солда́тъ soldier, ма́стеръ master, &c.
>
>    (2) *Inanimate* (неодушевлённый), *i.e.* those which have not life and voluntary motion. *Ex.* ду́бъ oak, до́мъ house, ко́мната room, перо́ feather.
>
>    *Obs.*—To the class of inanimate objects belong the *sensitive* (чу́вственный): *Ex.* бле́скъ splendour, го́речь bitterness, за́пахъ smell.
>
>    (3) *Intellectual* (у́мственный) or *abstract* (отвлечённый), which are presented to the understanding by such words as скро́мность modesty, прилежа́ніе application, воображе́ніе imagination, вре́мя time, го́дъ year, &c.
>
>    *Obs.*—Бо́гъ God, Богочеловѣ́къ godly man, а́нгелъ angel, ду́хъ spirit, душа́ soul, and other similar nouns which denote immaterial beings, are called *spiritual* (духо́вный) objects.

§ 23. Nouns Substantive are divided into (1) *appellative* (нарица́тельное), or *common* (о́бщее), under which denomination come all objects which are common to a class. *Ex.* человѣ́къ man, коро́ль king, го́родъ town, ра́дость joy, &c.

>    (2) *Proper* (со́бственное), by which we distinguish one object from all others that may be like it. *Ex.* Алекса́ндръ Alexander, Ма́рья Mary, Россі́я Russia, Во́лга Volga, &c.
>
>    *Obs.*—To the proper nouns belong not only all Christian names of people, but also their patronymics, and family

or surnames. *Ex.* Ивáновичъ son of John, Петрóвна daughter of Peter, Тургéневъ Toorgénéff, Пýшкинъ Pooshkin, &c.

(3) *Collective* (Собирáтельное), which by the use of one word imply few or many objects representing the same sort or kind. *Ex.* семéйство family, нарóдъ people, вóйско army, лѣсъ forest, &c.

*Obs.*—In order to note a quantity of animals, birds, or insects, the following collective nouns are used: стáдо herd or flock of cattle or sheep, табýнъ drove or stud of horses, стáя flight or covey of birds, or pack of dogs, рóй swarm of bees, &c.

(4) *Material* (вещéственное), which indicate the substance of the object, be the quantity large or small. *Ex.* зóлото gold, мѣдь copper, дéрево wood, мукá flour, мáсло oil, butter, &c.

§ 24. It is a peculiarity of the Russian language that nouns substantive may be (1) *augmentative* (увеличúтельное), or those which show the unusually large size of an object. *Ex.* солдáтище big soldier, ручúща large hand, столúще huge table, &c.

(2) *Diminutive* (уменьшúтельное), or those which designate the smallness of the object. *Ex.* солдáтикъ small soldier, рýчка small hand, стóликъ little table, &c.

To the class of diminutive nouns belong (a) the *complimentary* (привѣтственное) or *caressing* (ласкáтельное), which are used in the Russian language when addressing or naming favourite objects, or in order to give expression to a sense of love for such. *Ex.* брáтецъ dear brother, сестрúца dear sister, Вáня, Ванюша, Вáничка dear John, Катя, Катюша, Кáтенька dear Kate, лошáдушка dear horse, корóвушка dear cow, рýченька dear little hand, &c. (b) *Derogatory* (уничижúтельное), or those which give expression to a want of regard for an object, or a sense of its insignificance, or a contempt for it. *Ex.* книжóнка miserable book, домúшко wretched house, лошадёнка sorry horse, &c.

§ 25. In the case of nouns substantive the *gender* рóдъ, *number* числó, and *case* падéжъ, should be observed

§ 26. Nouns substantive in the Russian language have three *genders* (родъ), viz. *masculine* (мужескій), *feminine* (женскій), and *neuter* (средній).

 The gender of nouns substantive is ascertained either by their meaning or by their termination. As touching the former, all objects of the male sex (no matter what may be their termination) are of the masculine gender. *Ex.* слуга́ servant, дядя uncle, подмастёрье foreman, мѣня́ло money-changer, &c.; and objects of the female sex (no matter what may be their termination) belong to the feminine gender. *Ex.* служа́нка servant-maid, няня nurse, дочь daughter, &c.

 The same rule applies to animate objects which distinguish *male* (саме́цъ) and *female* (са́мка) in animals. *Ex.* левъ lion, льви́ца lioness, бара́нъ ram, овца́ ewe or sheep, пѣту́хъ cock, ку́рица hen, &c.

 Nouns ending in й and ъ belong to the masculine gender. *Ex.* мураве́й ant, орёлъ eagle, поко́й rest, сто́лъ table, &c.

 Nouns ending in а and я belong to the feminine gender. *Ex.* шпа́га sword, ли́лія lily, забо́та care, душа́ soul, &c.

 Nouns ending in о, е, and мя belong to the neuter gender. *Ex.* окно́ window, мо́ре sea, вре́мя time, &c.

 To the neuter gender belongs also дитя́ child.

 Of nouns substantive, which terminate in ь, some belong to the masculine gender. *Ex.* день day, кора́бль ship; whilst others belong to the feminine gender, as тѣнь shadow, пло́щадь plane, surface, &c.

§ 27. Besides the above, there are, in the Russian language, other nouns substantive ending in *a* and *я*, which are of the *common* (о́бщій) gender. In other words, such nouns as have the same termination for both masculine and feminine genders. *Ex.* сирота́ orphan, бродя́га vagabond, пла́кса whiner, родня́ kindred, &c.

§ 28. Augmentative and diminutive nouns, no matter what may be their terminations, belong to the gender of those nouns from which they are derived.

§ 29. Foreign nouns employed in the Russian language which end in *u* and *y*, when they denote animate objects, are of the masculine gender, and when they refer to inanimate or abstract objects are of the neuter gender. *Ex.* колибри humming-bird, какаду cockatoo, which are of the masculine gender: пари = закладъ bet, wager, which is of the neuter gender.

§ 30. Personal nouns have two genders, viz. masculine and feminine. *Ex.* Императоръ Emperor, Императрица Empress, Генералъ General, Генеральша General's wife, монахъ monk, монахиня nun, сосѣдъ male neighbour, сосѣдка female neighbour, &c. Директриса directress, инспектриса inspectress, экономка housekeeper, refer solely to the persons of the female sex who perform the duties indicated by their respective designations; whereas, on the other hand, директорша, инспекторша, экономша are the Russian designations for the wives of a director, inspector, and house steward respectively.

With regard to the names of peoples, the feminine is derived from the masculine thus:—from Россіянинъ Russian (man), comes Россіянка Russian (woman); from Англичанинъ Englishman, Англичанка Englishwoman; from Нѣмецъ German (man), we get Нѣмка German (woman), &c.

Personal nouns which denote kindred or affinity have for each sex separate denominations:—

Отецъ father, Мать mother.
Сынъ son, Дочь daughter.
Братъ brother, Сестра sister.
Дядя uncle, Тётка aunt.

§ 31. In the Russian language the denominations of the several degrees of relationship are extremely numerous. It may be well to observe the following:—

Тесть father-in-law, wife's father.
Тёща mother-in-law, wife's mother.
Шуринъ brother-in-law, wife's brother.
Свойчина or Свойченица sister-in-law, wife's sister.
Свойкъ brother-in-law, wife's sister's husband.
Свёкоръ father-in-law, husband's father.
Свекровь mother-in-law, husband's mother.
Деверь or Деверь brother-in-law, husband's brother.
Золовка sister-in-law, husband's sister.
Зять son-in-law or brother-in-law, daughter's husband or sister's husband.

Невѣстка daughter-in-law or sister-in-law, son's wife or brother's wife.
Отчимъ or Вотчимъ stepfather.
Мачиха stepmother.
Пасынокъ stepson.
Падчерица stepdaughter.

§ 32. There are two *numbers* (числó). The *singular* (едиственное), which speaks of one object: *Ex.* братъ brother, рѣка river. The *plural* (множественное), which refers to two or more objects of the same sort: *Ex.* братья brothers, рѣки rivers, &c.

§ 33. Certain nouns substantive are used in the singular number *only*, whilst others, although referring to one object, have only a plural form.

Of the former class there are (1) the greater part of the *proper* (собственное) nouns: *Ex.* Римъ Rome, Везувій Vesuvius, &c. (2) the greater number of the *material* (вещественное) nouns: *Ex.* золото gold, молоко milk, &c. (3) the names of the virtues and the vices: *Ex.* терпѣніе patience, лѣность indolence, &c. (4) many of the *abstract* (отвлеченное) nouns: *Ex.* счастіе fortune, старость old age, &c. (5) many of the names of plants, especially of the kitchen-garden: *Ex.* щавель sorrel, лукъ onion, &c.

Of the latter class some have meanings different to that of the singular form: *Ex.* люди people, ножницы pair of scissors, ворота gate, &c. Others are the names of old towns and places: *Ex.* Аѳины Athens, Ѳермопилы Thermopylæ, &c.

§ 34. Certain nouns have in the singular number one signification, and in the plural another. *Ex.* вѣсъ weight, вѣсы scales, деньга ¼ copeck, деньги money, часъ hour, часы watch, clock, &c.

§ 35. *Cases* (падежъ) are the terminations of nouns which show the various relations in which objects stand to each other.

§ 36. In the Russian language there are seven *cases*. They answer to certain questions:—

(1) *Nominative* (именительный), which answers to the questions—кто? who? что? what?[1] *Ex.* Кто пришёлъ? (past tense of verb придти), *who* came? *Ans.* Братъ brother. Что у тебя въ рукахъ? *What* is there (or hast thou) in (thy) hands? *Ans.* шляпа a hat.

(2) *Vocative* (звательный), which has its termination like the nominative, points to the designation of the object to which we refer. *Ex.* Братъ! поди[2] сюда. *Brother!* come here. Здоровъ-ли ты, любезный другъ? Art thou well, *dear friend?*

(3) *Genitive* (родительный), which answers to the questions—Кого? Чего? Чей? Чья? Чье? Of whom? Of which *or* of what? Whose (*masc. fem. neuter*)? *Ex.* Кого здѣсь нѣтъ?[3] *Who* is not here? *Ans.* Брата, brother.—Чего здѣсь нѣтъ? *What* is not here? *Ans.* Шляпы, the hat.—Чей этотъ домъ? *Whose* house (is) this? *Ans.* Моего приятеля, My friend's.

(4) *Dative* (дательный), which answers to the questions—Кому? Чему? To whom? To which? *or* to what? *Ex.* Кому ты отдалъ[4] книгу? *To whom* didst thou give back the book? *Ans.* Брату, To the brother.—Чему ты удивляешься?[5] *What* dost thou admire? *Ans.* шляпѣ the hat.

(5) *Accusative* (винительный), which answers to the questions—Кого? Что? whom? which? what? *Ex.* Кого ты видишь?[6] *Whom* dost thou see? *Ans.* брата brother. Что ты держишь?[7] *What* dost thou hold? *Ans.* шляпу the hat.

(6) *Instrumental* (творительный), which answers to the ques-

---

[1] The questions, Кто? Кого? Кому? Кѣмъ? О Комъ? serve for the animate nouns; whilst Что? Чего? Чему? Чѣмъ? О Чёмъ? are used in the cases of the inanimate and abstract nouns.

[2] Second person, singular number, imperative mood, of the verb пойти. *Trans.*

[3] With the impersonal verb нѣтъ the genitive case is required. *Trans.*

[4] Past tense of the verb отдать. *Trans.*

[5] Present tense of the verb удивляться, which governs the dative. *Trans.*

[6] Present tense of the verb видѣть. *Trans.*

[7] Present tense of the verb держать. *Trans.*

tions—Кѣмъ? Чѣмъ? by *whom?* by *what?* or by *which?* *Ex.* Кѣмъ ты доволенъ?[1] With *whom* art thou satisfied? *Ans.* Братомъ, with the brother.—Чѣмъ ты доволенъ? with *what,* or with *which,* art thou satisfied? *Ans.* шляпою, with the hat.

(7) *Prepositional* (предложный), which answers to the questions—о комъ? о чёмъ? при комъ? при чёмъ? на комъ? на чёмъ? въ комъ? въ чёмъ? about whom? about which, or what? near or at whom? near or at which or what? on whom? on which or what? in whom? in which or what? *Ex.* О комъ я говорю?[2] *about whom* do I speak? *Ans.* О братѣ, about brother.—О чёмъ я говорю? *about which* or *what* do I speak? *Ans.* О шляпѣ, about the hat.

*Obs.*—The nominative and vocative cases, the terminations of which are not subject to change (further than is caused by number), are called the *direct* (прямой) cases; whereas all the other cases, the terminations of which do alter (differing the one from the other), are called the *oblique* (косвенный) cases. The prepositional case is always used with *prepositions* (предлогъ). The following are the most frequently used prepositions:—о, or объ, or обо (about), на (on or upon), при (near, at, in the presence of), въ or во (in or at).

§ 37. The *declension* (склонéніе) of nouns marks the changes of termination which they undergo according to number and case. In the Russian language there are three declensions.

To the first belong those nouns substantive which terminate in ъ, й and ь, being of the masculine gender.

To the second those which terminate in *а* and *я,* of both the masculine and feminine genders, and those in *ь* of the feminine gender only.

To the third those which terminate in *о, е* and *мя,* being of the neuter gender.

§ 38. Nouns substantive are declined according to the following tables:—

---

[1] Abbreviated form of the adjective довóльный. *Trans.*

[2] Present tense of the verb говорúть. *Trans.*

( 11 )

*Singular Number.*

| Падеж.<br>Cases. | 1st DECLENSION.<br>MASC. TERMINATION. | | | 2nd DECLENSION.<br>FEM. TERMINATION. | | | 3rd DECLENSION.<br>NEUT. TERMINATION. | | |
|---|---|---|---|---|---|---|---|---|---|
| Имен. и Зват.<br>Nom. & Voc. | ъ | й | ь | а | я | ь | о | е | мя |
| Родит.<br>Gen. | а | я | я | ы | и | и | а | я | ени |
| Дат.<br>Dat. | у | ю | ю | ѣ | ѣ | и | у | ю | ени |
| Вин.<br>Acc. | { а<br>  ъ | я<br>й | я<br>ь } | у | ю | ь | о | о | мя |
| Твор.<br>Instr. | омъ | емъ | емъ | ою | ею | ью | омъ | емъ | енем |
| Пред.<br>Prep. | ѣ | ѣ | ѣ | ѣ | ѣ | и | ѣ | ѣ | ени |

*Plural Number.*

| Падеж.<br>Cases. | | | | | | | | | |
|---|---|---|---|---|---|---|---|---|---|
| Имен. и Зват.<br>Nom. & Voc. | ы | и | и | ы | и | и | а | я | ена |
| Родит.<br>Gen. | овъ | евъ | ей | ъ | ь | ей | ъ | ей | енъ |
| Дат.<br>Dat. | амъ | ямъ | ямъ | амъ | ямъ | ямъ | амъ | ямъ | енамъ |
| Вин.<br>Acc. | { овъ<br>  ы | евъ<br>и | ей<br>и } | { ъ<br>  ы | ь<br>и | ей<br>и } | а | я | ена |
| Твор.<br>Instr. | ами | ями | ями | ами | ями | ями | ами | ями | енами |
| Пред.<br>Prep. | ахъ | яхъ | яхъ | ахъ | яхъ | яхъ | ахъ | яхъ | енахъ |

## EXAMPLES OF THE FIRST DECLENSION.

*Singular Number.*

| | Animate Object. | Inanimate Object. | Inanimate Object. | Animate Object. |
|---|---|---|---|---|
| Н. З. | слонъ,<br>elephant. | столъ,<br>table. | покой,<br>rest, or room. | царь,<br>Tsar. |
| Р. | слона́,<br>of an elephant. | стола́,<br>of a table. | покоя,<br>of rest, &c. | царя́,<br>of a Tsar. |
| Д. | слону́,<br>to an elephant. | столу́,<br>to a table. | покою,<br>to rest, &c. | царю́,<br>to a Tsar. |
| В. | слона́,<br>an elephant. | столъ,<br>a table. | покой,<br>rest, &c. | царя́,<br>a Tsar. |
| Т. | слоно́мъ,<br>by an elephant. | столо́мъ,<br>by a table. | покоемъ,<br>with rest, &c. | царёмъ,<br>by a Tsar. |
| П. | о слонѣ,<br>about an elephant. | на столѣ,<br>on a table. | въ покоѣ,<br>at rest, &c. | при царѣ,<br>in the presence of<br>a Tsar. |

( 12 )

*Plural Number.*

| | Animate Object. | Inanimate Object. | Inanimate Object. | Animate Object. |
|---|---|---|---|---|
| И. З. | слоны́, elephants. | столы́, tables. | покóи, rooms. | цари́, Tsars. |
| Р. | слонóвъ, of elephants. | столóвъ, of tables. | покóевъ, of rooms. | царéй, of Tsars. |
| Д. | слонáмъ, to elephants. | столáмъ, to tables. | покóямъ, to rooms. | царя́мъ, to Tsars. |
| В. | слонóвъ, elephants. | столы́, tables. | покóи, rooms. | царéй, Tsars. |
| Т. | слонáми, by elephants. | столáми, by tables. | покóями, with rooms. | царя́ми, by Tsars. |
| П. | о слонáхъ, about elephants. | на столáхъ, on tables. | въ покóяхъ, in rooms. | при царя́хъ, in the presence of Tsars. |

*Singular Number.*

| | Animate Object. | Inanimate Object. | Inanimate Object. | Inanimate Object. |
|---|---|---|---|---|
| И. З. | льстéцъ, flatterer. | урожáй, crop. | трофéй, trophy. | гвоздь, nail. |
| Р. | льстецá, of a flatterer. | урожáя, of a crop. | трофéя, of a trophy. | гвоздя́, of a nail. |
| Д. | льстецý, to a flatterer. | урожáю, to a crop. | трофéю, to a trophy. | гвоздю́, to a nail. |
| В. | льстецá, a flatterer. | урожáй, a crop. | трофéй, a trophy. | гвоздь, a nail. |
| Т. | льстецóмъ, by a flatterer. | урожáемъ, by a crop. | трофéемъ, with a trophy. | гвоздёмъ, by a nail. |
| П. | о льстецé, about a flatterer. | объ урожáѣ, about a crop. | о трофéѣ, about a trophy. | о гвоздѣ́, about a nail. |

*Plural Number.*

| | Animate Object. | Inanimate Object. | Inanimate Object. | Inanimate Object. |
|---|---|---|---|---|
| И. З. | льстецы́, flatterers. | урожáи, crops. | трофéи, trophies. | гвóзди, nails. |
| Р. | льстецóвъ, of flatterers. | урожáевъ. of crops. | трофéевъ, of trophies. | гвоздéй, of nails. |
| Д. | льстецáмъ, to flatterers. | урожáямъ, to crops. | трофéямъ, to trophies. | гвоздя́мъ, to nails. |
| В. | льстецóвъ, flatterers. | урожáи, crops. | трофéи, trophies. | гвóзди, nails. |
| Т. | льстецáми, by flatterers. | урожáями, by crops. | трофéями, with trophies. | гвоздя́ми, by nails. |
| П. | о льстецáхъ, about flatterers. | объ урожáяхъ. about crops. | о трофéяхъ, about trophies. | о гвоздя́хъ, about nails. |

## EXAMPLES OF THE SECOND DECLENSION.

*Singular Number.*

|   | Animate Object. | Inanimate Object. | Inanimate Object. | Inanimate Object. |
|---|---|---|---|---|
| И. З. | ста́роста, headman. | звѣзда́, star. | пу́ля, bullet. | цѣпь, chain. |
| Р. | ста́росты, of a headman. | звѣзды́, of a star. | пу́ли, of a bullet. | цѣпи, of a chain. |
| Д. | ста́ростѣ, to a headman. | звѣздѣ́, to a star. | пу́лѣ, to a bullet. | цѣпи, to a chain. |
| В. | ста́росту, a headman. | звѣзду́, a star. | пу́лю, a bullet. | цѣпь, a chain. |
| Т. | ста́ростою, by a headman. | звѣздо́ю, by a star. | пу́лею, by a bullet. | цѣпью, with a chain. |
| П. | о ста́ростѣ, about a headman. | въ звѣздѣ́, in a star. | о пу́лѣ, about a bullet. | на цѣпи́, on a chain. |

*Plural Number.*

|   | | | | |
|---|---|---|---|---|
| И. З. | ста́росты, headmen. | звѣзды, stars. | пу́ли, bullets. | цѣпи, chains. |
| Р. | ста́ростъ, of headmen. | звѣздъ, of stars. | пуль, of bullets. | цѣпе́й, of chains. |
| Д. | ста́ростамъ, to headmen. | звѣздамъ, to stars. | пу́лямъ, to bullets. | цѣпя́мъ, to chains. |
| В. | ста́росту, headmen. | звѣзды, stars. | пу́ли, bullets. | цѣпи, chains. |
| Т. | ста́ростами, by headmen. | звѣздами, by stars. | пу́лями, by bullets. | цѣпя́ми, with chains. |
| П. | о ста́ростахъ, about headmen. | въ звѣздахъ, in stars. | о пу́ляхъ, about bullets. | въ цѣпя́хъ, in chains. |

*Singular Number.*

|   | Animate Object. | Animate Object. | Inanimate Object. | Inanimate Object. |
|---|---|---|---|---|
| И. З. | сирота́, orphan. | дя́дя, uncle. | недѣ́ля, week. | кисть, bunch, or wrist. |
| Р. | сироты́, of an orphan. | дя́ди, of an uncle. | недѣ́ли, of a week. | ки́сти, of a bunch, &c. |
| Д. | сиротѣ́, to an orphan. | дя́дѣ, to an uncle. | недѣ́лѣ, to a week. | ки́сти, to a bunch, &c. |
| В. | сироту́, an orphan. | дя́дю, an uncle. | недѣ́лю, a week. | кисть, a bunch, &c. |
| Т. | сирото́ю, by an orphan. | дя́дею, by an uncle. | недѣ́лею, by a week. | ки́стью, with a bunch, &c. |
| П. | о сиротѣ́, about an orphan. | при дя́дѣ, in the presence of an uncle. | въ недѣ́лѣ, in a week. | въ ки́сти, in a bunch, &c. |

## Plural Number.

| | Animate Object. | Animate Object. | Inanimate Object. | Inanimate Object. |
|---|---|---|---|---|
| И. З. | сиро́ты, orphans. | дя́ди, uncles. | педѣ́ли, weeks. | ки́сти, bunches, &c. |
| Р. | сиро́тъ, of orphans. | дя́дей, of uncles. | недѣ́ль, of weeks. | кистѣ́й, of bunches, &c. |
| Д. | сиро́тамъ, to orphans. | дя́дямъ, to uncles. | недѣ́лямъ, to weeks. | кистя́мъ, to bunches, &c. |
| В. | сиро́тъ, orphans. | дя́дей, uncles. | педѣ́ли, weeks. | ки́сти, bunches, &c. |
| Т. | сиро́тами, by orphans. | дя́дями, by uncles. | недѣ́лями, by weeks. | кистя́ми, with bunches, &c. |
| П. | о сиро́тахъ, about orphans. | при дя́дяхъ, in the presence of uncles. | въ недѣ́ляхъ, in weeks. | въ кистя́хъ, in bunches, &c. |

## EXAMPLES OF THE THIRD DECLENSION.

### Singular Number.

| | Inanimate Object. | Inanimate Object. | Inanimate Object. | Inanimate Object. |
|---|---|---|---|---|
| И. З. | дѣ́ло, affair. | о́бщество, society. | по́ле, field. | и́мя, name. |
| Р. | дѣ́ла, of an affair. | о́бщества, of society. | по́ля, of a field. | и́мени, of a name. |
| Д. | дѣ́лу, to an affair. | о́бществу, to society. | по́лю, to a field. | и́мени, to a name. |
| В. | дѣ́ло, an affair. | о́бщество, society. | по́ле, a field. | и́мя, a name. |
| Т. | дѣ́ломъ, with an affair. | о́бществомъ, by society. | по́лемъ, with a field. | и́менемъ, with a name. |
| П. | о дѣ́лѣ, about an affair. | въ о́бществѣ, in society. | на по́лѣ. in a field. | объ и́мени, about a name. |

### Plural Number.

| | Inanimate Object. | Inanimate Object. | Inanimate Object. | Inanimate Object. |
|---|---|---|---|---|
| И. З. | дѣла́, affairs. | о́бщества, societies. | поля́, fields. | имена́, names. |
| Р. | дѣлъ, of affairs. | о́бществъ, of societies. | поле́й, of fields. | имёнъ, of names. |
| Д. | дѣла́мъ, to affairs. | о́бществамъ, to societies. | поля́мъ, to fields. | именамъ, to names. |
| В. | дѣла́, affairs. | о́бщества, societies. | поля́, fields. | имена́, names. |
| Т. | дѣла́ми, by affairs. | о́бществами, by societies. | поля́ми, with fields. | именами, with names. |
| П. | о дѣла́хъ, about affairs. | въ о́бществахъ, in societies. | въ поля́хъ, in fields. | объ именахъ, about names. |

|      | Singular Number.                    |                                  | Plural Number.               |                                |
|------|-------------------------------------|----------------------------------|------------------------------|--------------------------------|
|      | Anim. or Inanim.                    | Inanimate Object.                | Anim. or Inanim.             | Inanimate Object.              |
| И. З.| лицо́, face, or person.              | зе́ркало, mirror.                 | ли́ца, faces, or persons.     | зеркала́, mirrors.              |
| Р.   | лица́, of a face, &c.                | зе́ркала, of a mirror.            | лиц, of faces, &c.           | зерка́л, of mirrors.            |
| Д.   | лицу́, to a face, &c.                | зе́ркалу, to a mirror.            | ли́цам, to faces, &c.         | зерка́лам, to mirrors.          |
| В.   | лицо́, a face, &c.                   | зе́ркало, a mirror.               | ли́ца, faces, &c.             | зеркала́, mirrors.              |
| Т.   | лицо́м, by a face, &c.               | зе́ркалом, with a mirror.         | ли́цами, by faces, &c.        | зерка́лами, with mirrors.       |
| П.   | на лице́, on a face, &c.             | в зе́ркале, in a mirror.          | о ли́цах, about faces, &c.    | в зерка́лах, in mirrors.        |

### § 39. *Rules for the Declensions.*

(1) Nouns substantive, taken from foreign languages, and which end in ъ, й and ь, are declined according to the first declension: *Ex.* сюже́тъ subject, антиква́рій antiquary, ве́ксель bill of exchange. Those which end in *a* and *я*, and also in *ь*, and which are of the feminine gender, are declined according to the second declension: *Ex.* фра́за phrase, а́рмія army, моде́ль model. Nouns taken from foreign languages, and which terminate in *o*, *e*, *u*, *y*, are not declined at all: *Ex.* депо́ depot, желе́ jelly, колибри humming-bird, какаду́ cockatoo, &c.

(2) The vowel ы is never found after the letters г, ж, к, х, ч, ш, щ: it is changed in such a case into *и*. For this reason the nominative case of the plural number of nouns which end in ъ are not quite according to the ordinary rule. *Ex.* враги́ enemies (from враг), ножи́ knives (from нож), чулки́ stockings (from чуло́к), духи́ spirits (from дух), ночи́ nights (from ночь), шалаши́ tents (from шала́ш), плащи́ cloaks (from плащ), &c., *instead* of враги, ножы, чулкы, &c. In like manner the genitive case of the singular number and the nominative case of the plural number of nouns ending in *a* are—кни́ги books (from кни́га), вельмо́жи grandees (from вельмо́жа), руки́ hands (from рука́), and *not* книгы, вельмо́жы, рукы, &c.

(3) After the same letters, too (г, ж, к, х, ч, ш, щ, and ц also), я and ю never follow. In place of я, *a* must be written, and in place of ю, *y*. *Ex.* In the genitive case singular we find се́рдца, and *not* се́рдця (from се́рдце, heart). So, too, in the dative case of the same

word we have сéрдцу, and *not* сéрдцю. Similarly the dative case of жилúще (dwelling) is жилúщу, and *not* жилúщю.

(4) Nouns substantive which end in *це* are declined after the manner of those which end in *о*, except that the instrumental case of the singular number, instead of омъ, has ёмъ. *Ex.* сéрдцемъ (from сéрдце heart), полотéнцемъ (from полотéнце towel), and the like. Those nouns which terminate in цо *accented* have in the instrumental case of the singular number *омъ*: *Ex.* яйцóмъ (from яйцó egg), лицóмъ (from лицó face, or person).

(5) All words containing the letters ж, ц, ч, ш, щ, which carry in the instrumental case of the singular number the *accent* (ударéніе) on the last syllable have омъ, and not емъ, for the termination of that case. *Ex.* ножóмъ (from ножъ knife), отцóмъ (from отéцъ father), &c. Similar words which *do not* carry the accent on the last syllable have емъ, and not омъ, for the termination of that case: *Ex.* мýжемъ (from мýжъ man, husband), мѣ́сяцемъ (from мѣ́сяцъ month), &c.

(6) In the declensions the letter *ѣ* never follows the letter *i*. Consequently, in the dative and prepositional cases of the singular number of nouns which end in *ія* it is necessary to write *и*, and not *ѣ*: *Ex.* Фрáнціи, to France (from Фрáнція); О лúліи, about a lily (from лúлія). The same rule is preserved in the prepositional case, singular number, of nouns which end in *iй* and *ie*. Thus При Антóніи, In the time of Anthony (from Антóній); Въ сочинéніи, in the composition (from сочинéніе); &c.

(7) Nouns feminine which terminate in *ь* also have in the dative and prepositional cases of the singular number *и*, and not *ѣ*: *Ex.* въ Сибúри, in Siberia (from Сибúрь), &c.

(8) In nouns masculine which terminate in *ь*, the genitive case of the singular number has *я*: *Ex.* день day, дня; звѣрь wild beast, звѣ́ря. In nouns of a like termination, but of the feminine gender, the termination of the same case of the same number has *и*: *Ex.* тѣнь shadow, тѣ́ни; дверь door, двéри. To the first part of this rule the following word is the sole exception: путь (road), which although of the masculine gender, has for the termination of its genitive case singular *и*, — thus, путú. Moreover, this word departs generally from the common rules laid down for the declensions. (*Vide* § 41.)

(9) A few nouns of the masculine gender ending in *ь* take, in the

nominative case of the plural number, the termination of the genitive case of the singular number—with this difference, that the accent is shifted to the last syllable: *Ex.* вексель bill of exchange, *plur.* векселя́; писарь writer, *plur.* писаря́, &c.

(10) In nouns substantive which terminate in *ie*, the nominative case of the plural number has я, and not и: *Ex.* желáнія wishes, (from желáніе), *not* желáніи, &c. The genitive case of the plural number of these nouns ends in *ій*, and *not* in *евъ*: *Ex.* желáній, and *not* желáніевъ, &c.

(11) Nouns substantive which terminate in *ія* also have in the genitive case of the plural number *ій*: *Ex.* лилія lily, лилій, &c.

(12) Nouns substantive which terminate in *ья* have in the genitive case of the plural number *ей*, for which reason the letter ь is dropped in the oblique cases: *Ex.* судьá judge, судéй, &c.

(13) Nouns substantive which end in *ея* and *ья* change in the genitive case of the plural number the final letter я into й: *Ex.* швея́ seamstress, швей; змѣя́ snake, змѣй, &c.

(14) Nouns which end in ъ, and in which the letters ж, ч, ш, щ are found, also have in the genitive case of the plural number *ей*: *Ex.* ножéй, (from ножъ); мечéй, (from мечъ); шалашéй, (from шалашъ); плащéй (from плащъ), &c.

(15) Nouns which end in *ще* have in the genitive case of the plural number ъ for their final termination: *Ex.* учи́лище school, учи́лищъ, &c.

(16) Nouns which terminate in *ко* have in the nominative case of the plural number и instead of *а* for their final letter: *Ex.* я́блоко apple, *plur.* я́блоки; but войско army, troops, and облако cloud, are exceptions to this rule, as we find войскá armies, облакá clouds.

(17) Many material nouns, of the masculine gender, which terminate in ъ, й, and ь, when placed after words denoting weight or measure, take in the genitive case of the singular number the termination of the dative case of the same number, *i.e.* take the final letters ю and у, instead of the letters peculiar to their proper terminations, viz. я and *а*. *Ex.* стакáнъ чáю (not чáя), from чай, cup of tea; аршинъ атлáсу (not атлáса), from атлáсъ, arsheen, or Russian ell, of satin, &c. When, however, the same nouns stand after words which do not express measure or weight, then the terminations of their genitive case (singular) are according to the

c

ordinary rule, *i.e.* in *a* and *я*, and not in *y* and *ю*: *Ex.* вкусъ чая, flavour of tea; нѣжность атласа, softness of satin, &c.

(18) The accusative case, singular number, of nouns of the masculine gender which terminate in ъ, й, ь, is, in the declension of the inanimate and abstract nouns, like the nominative; and, in that of the animate nouns, like the genitive. *Ex.* я вижу[1] (что?) столъ, столы́; ручéй, ручьи́; корáбль, корабли́—I see (*what?*) table, tables; brook, brooks; ship, ships. Я вижу (кого?) брáта, брáтьевъ; муравья́, муравёвъ; звѣря, зверéй—I see (*whom* or *what?*) brother, brothers; ant, ants; wild beast, wild beasts. The accusative case, singular number, of nouns of the masculine and feminine genders, which terminate in *a*, is in *y*: *Ex.* слугá, man-servant, слугу́; книга book, книгу. Similarly the accusative case, singular number, of nouns of the masculine and feminine genders, which terminate in *я*, is in *ю*: *Ex.* судья́ judge, судью́; пуля bullet, пу́лю. The accusative case, singular number, of nouns of the feminine gender, which terminate in ь, is always like the nominative. The same remark applies too to all nouns of the neuter gender, without any distinction. The accusative case, plural number, of nouns of any gender is, in the declension of the inanimate nouns, like the nominative, and in the declension of the animate nouns, like the genitive.

> *Obs.*—Collective nouns, even though they may denote a collection of animate objects of either the masculine or neuter genders, are declined in the accusative case like the inanimate nouns: *Ex.* Онъ разбилъ[2] непріятельскій полкъ, He defeated the enemy's regiment; Пастýхъ пригнáлъ[3] стáдо, The shepherd drove in the flock, &c.

(19) The Vocative is, as a general rule, like the nominative; yet in certain nouns it has a peculiar termination of its own, borrowed from the Church Slavonic tongue: *Ex.* Богъ God, *voc.* Бóже; Отéцъ Father, *voc.* Отче, &c.

(20) Nouns which terminate in *мя* change *я* in all the oblique cases of both numbers into *e*: *Ex.* врéмя time, врéмени; врéменемъ, &c. One word alone with this primary termination of *мя*

---

[1] Present tense of the verb видѣть. *Trans.*
[2] Past tense of the verb разбить. *Trans.*
[3] Past tense of the verb пригнáть. *Trans.*

retains in the genitive case, plural number, the letter я: this word is сѣмя seed, сѣмянъ of seeds.

(21) The words нѐбо heaven, and чудо miracle, in the cases of the plural number have nom. небеса́, чудеса́; gen. небе́съ, чуде́съ, and so on. But when by the use of the word чудо is understood чудовище monster, чудо forms its plural thus, чуды, чудъ, чу-дамъ, &c.

(22) The following nouns and a few others form their genitive case plural like their nominative case singular; in other words, there is no change in form between the two cases: *Ex.* человѣкъ, man (or of men); солдатъ, soldier (or of soldiers)'; драгунъ, dragoon (or of dragoons); гусаръ, hussar (or of hussars); уланъ, Uhlan (or of Uhlans); кадетъ, cadet (or of cadets); Турокъ, Turk (or of Turks); гренадеръ, grenadier (or of grenadiers); рекрутъ, recruit (or of recruits); аршинъ, arsheen (or of arsheens); пудъ, pood (or of poods); чулокъ, stocking (or of stockings); сапогъ, boot (or of boots), and others. Hence it is not correct to speak of солда́товъ, гуса́ровъ, аршиновъ, пудо́въ, пулко́въ, сапого́въ, &c. The word са́жень (a sajen, or Rusian fathom) in the genitive case, plural number, has саже́нъ, and not са́жень or сажене́й.

(23) Certain nouns, which terminate in ъ and ь, take in the prepositional case of the singular number у or ю, instead of ѣ. In all such cases the accent falls on the final syllable: *Ex.* на боку́ on the side or flank, from бокъ; въ лѣсу́ in the forest, from лѣсъ; въ раю́ in Paradise, from рай; &c.

§ 40. The following are some examples of nouns substantive which depart from the ordinary rules of declension:—

(1) Nouns which terminate in анинъ and янинъ have in the plural number special terminations.

*Plural Number.*

| | (*Animate Objects.*) | (*Animate Objects.*) |
|---|---|---|
| N. & V. | И. 3. Англича́не, Englishmen. | Крестья́не, peasants. |
| G. | Р. Англича́нъ, of Englishmen. | Крестья́нъ, of peasants. |
| D. | Д. Англича́намъ, to Englishmen. | Крестья́намъ, to peasants. |
| A. | В. Англича́нъ, Englishmen. | Крестья́нъ, peasants. |
| I. | Т. Англича́нами, by Englishmen. | Крестья́нами, by peasants. |
| P. | П. Объ Англича́нахъ, about Englishmen. | О Крестья́нахъ, about peasants. |

*N.B.*—The *singular* number of nouns substantive terminating in анинъ and янинъ is declined according to the examples given of the first declension (*vide* paragraph 38).

(2) Nouns Substantive terminating in *ёнокъ* are declined in *both* numbers according to the following examples:

*Singular Number.*

|  |  | (Animate Objects.) | (Animate Objects.) |
|---|---|---|---|
| N. & V. | И. З. | Телёнокъ, calf. | Волчёнокъ, wolf's cub. |
| G. | Р. | Телёнка, of a calf. | Волчёнка, of a wolf's cub. |
| D. | Д. | Телёнку, to a calf. | Волчёнку, to a wolf's cub. |
| A. | В. | Телёнка, a calf. | Волчёнка, a wolf's cub. |
| I. | Т. | Телёнкомъ, by a calf. | Волчёнкомъ, by a wolf's cub. |
| P. | П. | О Телёнкѣ, about a calf. | О Волчёнкѣ, about a wolf's cub. |

*Plural Number.*

|  |  |  |  |
|---|---|---|---|
| N. & V. | И. З. | Телята, calves. | Волчата, wolf's cubs. |
| G. | Р. | Телятъ, of calves. | Волчатъ, of wolf's cubs. |
| D. | Д. | Телятамъ, to calves. | Волчатамъ, to wolf's cubs. |
| A. | В. | Телятъ, calves. | Волчатъ, wolf's cubs. |
| I. | Т. | Телятами, by calves. | Волчатами, by wolf's cubs. |
| P. | П. | О Телятахъ, about calves. | О Волчатахъ, about wolf's cubs. |

*N.B.*—According to the above two examples on *ёнокъ* are declined ребёнокъ, child, infant; жеребёнокъ, foal; ягнёнокъ, lamb; котёнокъ, kitten; поросёнокъ, sucking-pig; цыплёнокъ, chicken; медвѣнёнокъ, bear's cub. But львёнокъ, lion's whelp, and мышёнокъ, little mouse, respectively make their nominative case plural in енки; thus, львёнки and мышёнки, and *not* львята and мышата.

§ 41. The following nouns substantive depart altogether from the ordinary rules of declension :—

*Singular Number.*

|  | Animate Objects. | | Inanimate Objects. | |
|---|---|---|---|---|
| П. З. N.&V. | Дитя, child. | Мать, mother. | Церковь, church. | Путь, road. |
| Р. G. | Дитяти, of child. | Матери, of a mother. | Церкви, of a church. | Пути, of a road. |
| Д. D. | Дитяти, to a child. | Матери, to a mother. | Церкви, to a church. | Пути, to a road. |
| В. A. | Дитя, a child. | Мать, a mother. | Церковь, a church. | Путь, a road. |
| Т. I. | Дитятею, by child. | Матерью, by a mother. | Церковью, by a church. | Путёмъ, by a road. |
| П. P. | О Дитяти, about a child. | О Матери, about a mother. | Въ Церкви, in a church. | На Пути, on a road. |

*Plural Number.*

| | | | |
|---|---|---|---|
| П. 3. N. & V. | Дѣти, children. | Мáтери, mothers. | Церквú, churches. | Путú, roads. |
| P. G. | Дѣтéй, of children. | Матерéй, of mothers. | Церквéй, of churches. | Путéй, of roads. |
| Д. D. | Дѣтямъ, to children. | Матерямъ, to mothers. | Церквáмъ, to churches. | Путямъ, to roads. |
| В. A. | Дѣтéй, children. | Матерéй, mothers. | Церквú, churches. | Путú, roads. |
| Т. I. | Дѣтьмú, by children. | Матерямú, by mothers. | Церквáми, by churches. | Путями, with roads. |
| П. P. | О Дѣтяхъ, about children. | О Матеряхъ, about mothers. | В Церквáхъ, in churches. | О Путяхъ, about roads. |

*Obs.*—The word дочь (daughter) is declined like мать.

| | | | |
|---|---|---|---|
| N. И. | Хрпстóсъ, Christ. | | Госпóдь, Lord. |
| G. P. | Христá, of Christ. | | Гóспода, of the Lord. |
| D. Д. | Христý, to Christ. | | Гóсподу, to the Lord. |
| A. В. | Христá, Christ. | | Гóспода, the Lord. |
| V. З. | Христé! O Christ ! | | Гóсподи ! O Lord ! |
| I. Т. | Христóмъ, by Christ. | | Гóсподомъ, by the Lord. |
| P. П. | О Христѣ, about Christ. | | О Гóсподѣ, about the Lord. |

§ 42. The following words have special inflections both in the genitive case singular, in the other oblique cases of that number, and in all the cases of the plural number :—

(1) By changing the intermediate letter *e* of the nominative case singular into *ь* :—

    *Ex.*  Левъ, lion, льва.      Воробéй, sparrow, воробья́.
           Лёдъ, ice, льда.        Муравéй, ant, муравья́.
           Лёнъ, flax, льна.       Соловéй, nightingale, соловья́.
           Ручéй, brook, ручья́.    Жилéцъ, tenant, жильца́.
           Улéй, beehive, улья́.    Дѣлéцъ, statesman, дѣльца́, &c.

(2) By changing the intermediate letter *e* of the nominative case singular into *й* :—

    *Ex.*  Наёмъ, rent, найма,    Перешéекъ, isthmus, перешéйка.
           Заёмъ, loan, займа.      Боéцъ, gladiator, бойца, &c.

(3) By changing the intermediate letter *я* of the nominative case singular into *й* :—

          *Ex.*    Зáяцъ, hare, зáйца, &c.

(4) By the elision of the letter *e* of the nominative case singular :—

*Ex.* Молéбенъ, Te Deum, Молéбна.
Пáвелъ, Paul, Пáвла.
Орёлъ, eagle, орлá.
Котéлъ, kettle, котлá.
Узелъ, note, узлá.
Пéпелъ, ashes, пéпла.
Козёлъ, he-goat, козлá.
Осёлъ, jackass, donkey, ослá.
Купéцъ, merchant, купцá.
Отéцъ, father, отцá.
Кáмень, stone, кáмня.
Пень, stump, blockhead, пня.
День, day, дня.
Ремéнь, strap, ремня́.

Ковёръ, carpet, коврá.
Вéтеръ, wind, вéтра.
Шатёръ, tent, шатрá.
Костёръ, funeral pile, костра.
Хребéтъ, spine, or ridge, хребтá.
Егúпетъ, Egypt, Егúпта.
Овёсъ, oats, овсá.
Пёсъ, dog, пса.
Агнецъ, lamb, áгнца.
Самодéржецъ, autocrat, самодéржца.
Стéбель, stalk, стéбля.
Кáшель, cough, кáшля.
Сéлезень, drake, сéлезня.

(5) By the elision of the letter *o* of the nominative case singular:—

Сонъ, sleep, сна.
Огонь, fire, огня́.
Псалóмъ, psalm, псалмá.
Уголъ, corner, углá.
Уголь, charcoal, у́гля.
Угорь, pimple, угря́.
Лобъ, forehead, лба.
Посóлъ, ambassador, послá.
Чехóлъ, cover, чехлá.
Хохóлъ, crest, tuft of hair, хохлá.
Багóръ, harpoon, багрá.
Бугóръ, hillock, бугрá.

Вихоръ, tuft of hair, вúхра.
Свёкоръ, father-in-law, husband's father, свёкра.
Ротъ, mouth, рта.
Зáмокъ, castle, зáмка.
Нóготь, nail, нóгтя.
Дёготь, tar, pitch, дёгтя.
Зовъ, call, invitation, зва.
Шовъ, seam, шва.
Участокъ, share, участка.
Ломóть, slice, ломтя́.
Лóкоть, elbow, лóктя.
Чулóкъ, stocking, чулкá.

Also many other words terminating in окъ.

§ 43. The following words have special terminations for the nominative case of the plural number:—

óко, eye, óчи.
у́хо, ear, у́ши.
рукáвъ, sleeve, рукавá.
лéкарь, physician, лекаря́.
глазъ, eye, глазá.
бояринъ, boyard, бояре.
бáринъ, gentleman, master, бáре.
господúнъ, lord, master, mister, господá.

хозяинъ, master of the house, хозя́ева.
шу́ринъ, brother-in-law, wife's brother, шурья́.
братъ, brother, брáтья.
кумъ, Godfather, a gossip, кумовья́.
другъ, friend, друзья́.
князь, prince, князья́.
сóлнце, sun, сóлнца.
перó, pen, пéрья.

The following nouns have two terminations in the nominative case of the plural number:—домъ house, *plur.* домá and домы́; учитель tutor, *plur.* учителя́ and учители; профéссоръ professor, *plur.* профессора́ and профе́ссоры. The first of these terminations is in each instance the more frequently used in the language of conversation, and the latter in literature.

The following nouns (and others which by practice can easily be ascertained) have the termination of the nominative case of the plural number in *ья* :—

 стулъ, chair, сту́лья; прутъ, twig, rod, пру́тья; сукъ, branch, bough, су́чья.

§ 44. The following nouns have in the plural number double terminations, conveying in each instance different meanings :—

| | |
|---|---|
| вѣкъ, вѣки, eyelids. | вѣка́, centuries. |
| хлѣбъ, хлѣ́бы, loaves. | хлѣба́, grain of various kinds. |
| цвѣтъ, цвѣты́, flowers. | цвѣта́, colours. |
| зубъ, зу́бы, teeth in the mouth. | зу́бья, teeth of a comb or of a saw. |
| мѣхъ, мѣхи́, pair of bellows. | мѣха́, furs of all kinds. |
| листъ, листы́, leaves of a book, sheets of paper. | ли́стья, leaves of a tree. |
| мужъ, мужи́, men. | мужья́, husbands. |
| сынъ, сыновья́, sons. | сыны́, sons of the fatherland only. |

In the case of the following words :—

 де́рево, tree or wood, дерева́, дере́вья.
 ка́мень, stone, ка́мни, каме́нья.
 у́голь, charcoal, у́гли, уго́лья.
 ко́рень, root, ко́рни, коре́пья.
 крюкъ, hook, crook, крюки́, крю́чья.

The latter termination is used in a collective sense only.

колѣ́но (knee) has for its plural колѣ́ни and колѣ́на, the last signifying race or generation.

§ 45. The following nouns have special terminations in the genitive case of the plural number :—

| | | | |
|---|---|---|---|
| In *ебъ*, | сва́дьба, wedding, | *genitive plur.* | сва́дебъ. |
| | су́дьба, fate, destiny, | ,, | су́дебъ. |
| | тя́жба, lawsuit, | ,, | тя́жебъ. |
| In *егъ*, | де́ньги, copeck, | ,, | де́негъ. |
| | серьги́, earring, | ,, | серёгъ. |
| In *огъ*, | ро́зга, rod, | ,, | ро́зогъ. |
| In *екъ*, | ше́йка, finger-board, | ,, | ше́екъ. |
| | лю́лька, cradle, | ,, | лю́лекъ. |
| | ня́нька, nurse-maid, | ,, | ня́некъ. |
| | ло́жка, spoon, | ,, | ло́жекъ. |
| | ру́чка, small hand, handle, | ,, | ру́чекъ. |
| | коле́чко, ring, link, | ,, | коле́чекъ. |
| | око́шко, little window, | ,, | око́шекъ. |

And so too have other nouns whose nominative case singular ends in чко and шко.

| | | | |
|---|---|---|---|
| In *окъ*, | свя́зка, bundle, | gen. plur. | свя́зокъ. |
| | ба́бка, grandmother, midwife. | „ | ба́бокъ. |
| | доска́, board, plank, | „ | досо́къ. |
| | па́лка, stick, | „ | па́локъ. |
| In *елъ*, | метла́, broom, | „ | мете́лъ. |
| | се́дло, saddle | „ | се́делъ. |
| | весло́, ear, | „ | ве́селъ. |
| | ремесло́, trade, craft, | „ | реме́селъ. |
| | число́, number, | „ | чи́селъ. |
| In *алъ*, | зе́ркало, mirror, | „ | зерка́лъ. |
| In *олъ*, | ку́кла, doll, | „ | ку́колъ. |
| | зло, evil, | „ | золъ. |

(This word is used in the genitive case *only* of the plural number.)

| | | | |
|---|---|---|---|
| | стекло́, glass, *i.e.* pane of glass, and mirror glass, | gen. plur. | стёколъ. |
| | игла́, needle, | „ | и́голъ. |
| In *елъ*, | кро́вля, roof, | „ | кро́вель. |
| | ка́пля, drop, | „ | ка́пель. |
| | са́бля, a sabre, | „ | са́бель. |
| | пе́тля, noose, | „ | пете́ль. |
| | земля́, earth, | „ | земе́ль. |
| In *емъ*, | письмо́, letter, | „ | пи́семъ. |
| | тюрьма́, prison, | „ | тю́ремъ. |
| | корчма́, inn, | „ | корче́мъ. |
| | тьма, darkness, | „ | темъ. |

(When тьма means number. In the Ancient Slavonic reckoning this word signified *ten thousand*.)

| | | | |
|---|---|---|---|
| In *енъ*, | бревно́, beam, | genitive plur. | брёвенъ. |
| | сосна́, fir-tree, | „ | со́сенъ. |
| | зерно́, grain, kernel, | „ | зёренъ. |
| | бо́йня, slaughter-house, | „ | бо́енъ. |
| | полотно́, linen, | „ | поло́тенъ. |
| | купа́льня, bathing-place, | „ | купа́ленъ. |
| | су́дно, vessel, | „ | су́денъ. |
| | спа́льня, bedroom, | „ | спа́ленъ. |
| | гри́вна, ten copeck-piece, | „ | гри́венъ. |
| | вече́рня, vespers, | „ | вече́ренъ. |
| | Царе́вна, title of the Russian Imperial Princess, | „ | Царе́венъ. |
| | обе́дня, Mass, | „ | обе́денъ. |
| | княжна́, unmarried Princess, | „ | Княже́нъ. |
| | пе́сня, song, | „ | пе́сенъ. |
| | тамо́жня, custom-house, | „ | тамо́женъ. |
| | ба́сня, tale, a story, | „ | ба́сенъ. |
| | ви́шня, cherry-tree, | „ | ви́шенъ. |
| | ба́шня, tower, | „ | ба́шенъ. |

| In *ень*, | деревня, village, hamlet, | ,, | деревень. |
| | рудокопня, mine, | ,, | рудокопень. |
| | хлѣбня, bake-house, | ,, | хлѣбень. |
| | камено-ломня, quarry, | ,, | камено-ломень. |
| In *онъ*, | кухня, kitchen, | ,, | кухонъ. |
| | окно, window, | ,, | оконъ. |
| | сукно, cloth, | ,, | суконъ. |
| In *ерь*, | сестра, sister, | ,, | сестёръ. |
| | ведро, pail, | ,, | ведеръ. |
| | ядро, kernel, | ,, | ядеръ. |
| | ребро, rib, | ,, | реберъ. |
| In *ецъ*, | полотенце, towel, | ,, | полотенецъ. |
| | овца, sheep, ewe, | ,, | овецъ. |
| | кольцо, ring, | ,, | колецъ. |
| | сердце, heart, | ,, | сердецъ. |
| | крыльцо, flight of steps, | ,, | крылецъ. |

*N.B.*—The genitive case, plural, of кушанье food, is кушаньевъ, and of помѣстье an estate помѣстій.

§ 46. Nouns which are used in the plural number only are declined, if of the masculine gender, according to the first declension; if of the feminine gender, according to the second declension; and if of the neuter gender, according to the third declension. The gender of such nouns is ascertainable by their nominative and genitive cases:—

(1) Nouns which terminate in the nominative case in *ы* or *и*, and in the genitive in *евъ* or *овъ*, are of the masculine gender. *Ex.* щипцы́, pair of tongs, щипцо́въ; тиски́, press, vice, тиско́въ; обо́и, hangings, tapestry, обо́евъ. The following is an exception: око́вы, chains, fetters, око́въ. This noun is of the feminine gender.

(2) Any other nouns which terminate in the nominative case in *ы* or *и*, and in the genitive case in any sort of termination, are all of the feminine gender. *Ex.* са́ни, sledge, сане́й; но́жницы, pair of scissors, но́жницъ; сли́вки, cream, сли́вокъ. The following is an exception: лю́ди, people, люде́й. This noun is of the masculine gender.

(3) Nouns which terminate in the nominative case of the plural number in *а* are of the neuter gender. *Ex.* ворота́, gate; дрова́, wood; уста́, lips, mouth.

## Concerning the Declension of Compound Nouns.

§ 47. In compound nouns the last word alone is declined. *Ex.* мореходецъ, navigator, морехо́дца, морехо́дцу, &c.

§ 48. Certain proper nouns have their own peculiar appositions: *Ex.* Ричáрдъ Львúное Сéрдце, Richard *Lion-hearted*. In all such instances the proper name only is declined, the noun or nouns in apposition remaining without change: *Ex.* Ричáрдомъ Львúное Сéрдце, by Richard *Lion-hearted*; О Ричáрдѣ Львúное Сéрдце, about Richard *Lion-hearted*.

§ 49. The following compound nouns, which used to be declined separately, are now only inflected in the latter word:—Царьгрáдъ, Tsar's City (name given by the Russians to Constantinople), Царьгрáда, &c.; Нóвгородъ, New City (Novgorod), Нóвгорода, &c.

§ 50. Nouns substantive, to which is prefixed the word *полъ* or *полу* (contracted from *половúна*, half), have in all the oblique cases *полу*: *Ex.* пóлдень mid-day, *gen.* полýдня, *dat.* полýдню, *ins.* полýднемъ, *prep. о* полýднѣ.

### The Noun Adjective (имя прилагáтельное).

§ 51. Nouns adjective are coupled with nouns substantive, in order to show the quality, attributes, and circumstances of the object. Nouns adjective agree with the substantives with which they are coupled in gender, number and case. *Ex.* хрáбрый вóинъ, brave warrior; хрáбрые вóины, brave warriors; хрáбрыхъ вóиновъ, of brave warriors; бѣлая лóшадь, white horse; золотáя шпáга, golden sword; здѣшнее óбщество, local society; &c.

§ 52. Nouns adjective are comprised under the following heads:—

(1) *Qualifying* (кáчественное), which denote the quality or property of the several objects with which they are coupled. *Ex.* хрáбрый, brave; высóкiй, high; мáлый, little, small; &c.

(2) *Possessive* (притяжáтельное), which point out either to what the object belongs, such as Россíйскiй Russian, and львúный pertaining to a lion, &c.; or the substance of which the object is made, or to which it relates—for example, золотóй golden, кáменный, of stone.

*N.B.*—The possessive adjectives are formed from nouns substantive.

(3) *Circumstantial* (обстоятельственное), which point to the dependence of the object on the circumstances of time and place. *Ex.* сегодняшный урокъ, lesson of to-day; вчерашнiй обѣдъ, dinner of yesterday; здѣшнее общество, local society; &c.

§ 53. Nouns adjective have seven terminations, viz. for masculine gender, in *ый, ой, iй*; for feminine gender, in *ая, яя*; for neuter gender, in *oe, ee*.

*Ex.* Masc. славный ⎫  худой ⎫  синiй ⎫
Fem. славная ⎬ renowned,  худая ⎬ bad,  синяя ⎬ blue.
Neut. славное ⎭  худое ⎭  синее ⎭

§ 54. All nouns adjective are subject to changes of termination in connection with the ordinary rules of declension. The qualifying adjectives are moreover influenced by changes of termination, connected with the use of shortened (усѣчéнный) forms, and with the *degrees of comparison* (степéнь сравнéнiя).

§ 55. The *shortening* (усѣчéнie) amounts to a contraction of the full termination of the adjective in question. For example, instead of велúкiй -ая -ое, great, велúкъ-á-о are the forms used.

§ 56. Qualifying adjectives have, therefore, for every case and number, two distinct terminations, viz. the *full* (пóлное) and the *shortened* (усѣчéнное).

§ 57. The possessive and the circumstantial adjectives, on the other hand, have but the one *full* termination. *Ex.*, человѣческiй -ая -ое human, бумáжный -ая -ое made of paper, здѣшнiй -яя -ее belonging to this place.

*Obs.*—Certain of the *possessive* adjectives, which are derived from *personal* nouns, may have *two* distinct terminations; such as,—

| | | | | | |
|---|---|---|---|---|---|
| The full, | цáрскiй -ая -ое ⎫ | belonging to | дѣдовскiй -ая -ое ⎫ | belonging to |
| or | | the Tsar. | | one's ancestors. |
| The shortened, | царéвъ éва éво ⎭ | | дѣдовъ -ова -ово ⎭ | |
| The full, | отцóвскiй -ая -ое ⎫ | patrimonial. | брáтнiй -яя -ее ⎫ | fraternal. |
| or | | | брáтнинъ -нина | |
| The shortened, | отцóвъ -óва -óво ⎭ | | -нино ⎭ | |

§ 58. The shortened terminations of adjectives are as follows:—

(1) Of the qualifying adjectives—

|    | Singular Number. | | | Plural Number. |
|----|----|----|----|----|
|    | Masc. | Fem. | Neuter. | All genders. |
| In | ъ, ь. | а, я. | о, е. | ы, и. |

*Ex.* добръ kind, добра́, добро́, добры́;
синь blue, синя́, сине́, сини́.

(2) Of the possessive adjectives (derived from personal nouns)—
евъ, овъ, инъ; ева, ова, ина; ево, ово, ино; евы, овы, ины.

*Ex.* царе́въ, царе́ва, царе́во, царе́вы;
дѣ́довъ, дѣ́дова, дѣ́дово, дѣ́довы.
зя́тнинъ, зя́тнина, зя́тнино, зя́тнины.

§ 59. The degrees of comparison of nouns adjective denote the various standards of the quality or property of an object. *Ex.* у́мный learned, умнѣ́е or умнѣ́йшій more learned, and са́мый у́мный most learned; чёрный black, чернѣ́е or чернѣ́йшій blacker, and весьма́ чёрный blackest of all, *lit.* very black; сла́бый weak, слабѣ́е or слабѣ́йшій weaker, and са́мый сла́бый weakest. The degrees of comparison are three:—

(1) *Positive* (положи́тельная), which indicates the simple quality or property of an object, without making any comparison between it and any other object which may possess a like quality or property. *Ex.* ва́жный чинъ important rank; высо́кая гора́, high mountain; &c.

(2) *Comparative* (сравни́тельная), which intimates, in a greater or less degree, the quality or property of one object as compared with one or more objects of the same sort. *Ex.* Вы избра́ли важнѣ́йшую до́лжность не́жели онъ, You have chosen *a more important* duty (or office) than he; Это сукно́ чернѣ́е не́жели твое́, This cloth (is) *blacker* than thine; Братъ мой вы́ше тебя́, My brother (is) *taller* than thee; &c.

(3) *Superlative* (превосхо́дная), which points out the object possessed of the greatest degree of superiority or inferiority amongst a lot of objects of the same kind. *Ex.* Онъ чита́етъ са́мую поле́зную кни́гу, He is reading a *most useful* book; Вотъ са́мое чёрное сукно́, Here is the *blackest* cloth (of all); &c.

§ 60. Nouns Adjective have in the comparative degree two distinct terminations, viz. a full termination in *ѣйшій -ая -ее* and *айшій -ая -ее*, and a shortened termination in *ѣе, ѣй, же, че, ше, ще*. *Ex.* сильнѣйшій stronger, сильнѣе, сильнѣй; глубочайшій deeper, глу́бже; ле́гче lighter; ти́ше quieter; сла́ще sweeter.

> *Obs.*—The terminations *ѣйшій* and *айшій* may be used to express the superlative degree, but when so employed the words *изъ всѣхъ*, of all, must be understood. *Ex.* Россі́я есть сильнѣ́йшее госуда́рство въ свѣ́тѣ, Russia is *the most powerful* sovereignty in the world.

§ 61. The superlative degree is formed—

(1) By placing before the full termination of either the positive or comparative degree the words—*са́мый* most, *пре* very. *Ex.* Са́мый пріа́тный день, Most pleasant day; Са́мая высоча́йшая гора́, Highest mountain (of all); Прекра́сный цвѣто́къ, Prettiest flower.

(2) By placing before the full termination of the positive degree the words *весьма́* extremely, *о́чень* very. *Ex.* Весьма́ поле́зное изобрѣте́ніе, Extremely useful invention; О́чень пріа́тная встрѣ́ча, Very pleasant meeting.

(3) By prefixing to certain adjectives of the comparative degree the particle *наи*, very best. *Ex.* Наилу́чшій спо́собъ, very best method; *наибо́лѣе поле́зное дѣло*, much the more useful work.

§ 62. For further intensifying the comparative degree the following word can be placed before the *shortened* termination of that degree—*гора́здо* much. *Ex.* Онъ гора́здо умнѣе, но гора́здо ху́же, He (is) *much* more clever, but *much* worse than, &c.

For the purpose of detracting from the quality of an adjective the particle *по* (little) can be prefixed to the comparative degree of the adjective in question. *Ex.* Онъ посильнѣе васъ, He (is) *a little* stronger (than) you; &c.

§ 63. The following nouns adjective have their own peculiar forms of the degrees of comparison:—

|  | Full. | Comparative. Shortened. | Superlative. |
|---|---|---|---|
| вели́кій great, *in the sense of famous,* | } | | |
| большо́й great, *in the sense of large,* | бо́льшій, | бо́лѣе & бо́льше, | величайшій. |
| ма́лый small, | ме́ньшій, | ме́нѣе & ме́ньше, | малѣйшій. |
| высо́кій tall, | вы́сшій, | вы́ше, | высоча́йшій. |
| ни́зкій lower, | ни́зшій, | ни́же, | нижа́йшій. |
| хоро́шій good, | лу́чшій, | лу́чше, | наилу́чшій. |
| худо́й bad, | ху́дшій, | ху́же, | наиху́дшій. |
| ста́рый old, | старѣ́йшій, | ста́рѣе & ста́рше, | ста́ршій. |
| молодо́й young, | } | моло́же, | мла́дшій. |
| до́лгій long, | *nil* | до́лѣе & до́льше, | должа́йшій. |
| кра́ткій short, | } | коро́че, | кратча́йшій. |

§ 64. *Qualifying* nouns adjective can be used either in a *depreciative* or *softened* (смягчи́тельный) sense, with either full or shortened terminations; or in an *augmentative* (усиленный) form, with either full or shortened terminations.

*Ex.*     **Depreciative or Softened.**

Full termination . . { бѣленькій до́микъ, little white house;
{ бѣлова́тый домъ, whitish house;

Shortened termination { домъ бѣлёнокъ, the house (is) a little white;
{ домъ бѣлова́тъ, the house (is) whitish.

**Augmentative.**

Full termination . . . бѣлёховькій домъ, very white house;
Shortened termination . бѣлёхонекъ домъ or бѣлёшенекъ, the house (is) quite white.

§ 65. Certain nouns adjective are used in the sense of *appellative* (нарица́тельное) nouns substantive. *Ex.* вы́борный, deputy (*lit.* one chosen); часово́й, sentry; гости́ная (ко́мната), drawing-room; столо́вая (ко́мната), dining-room; жарко́е, roast meat.

Again, other nouns adjective are converted into surnames, and are used as proper names. *Ex.* Толсто́й, Tolstói; Задуна́йскій, *of Trans*-Danube; &c.

§ 66. Certain of the qualifying nouns adjective have no degrees of comparison at all; for instance, нѣмо́й dumb, слѣпо́й blind, жена́тый married; and such other adjectives the meaning of which will not admit of an increasing or diminishing of their peculiar significations.

§ 67. To many adjectives which denote quality of a good kind the particles *не* not, and *без* without, can be prefixed. This process has the effect of giving to the adjectives so treated a contrary signification to that which they previously held. *Ex.* Непрія́тный *dis*agreeable, нечи́стый *un*clean, безси́льный power*less*, &c.

> *Obs.*—The particle *без*, which is called a preposition, signifies deprivation, or the want of possession of anything, no matter what. Hence many adjectives which primarily indicate bad qualities when joined with this particle or preposition, come to express on the other hand good qualities. *Ex.* Безвре́дный harm*less*, безопа́сный *safe*, &c.

§ 68. Certain nouns adjective, which are derived from one and the same word, may, according to their meaning, appear in two forms, viz. be either possessive or qualifying adjectives. *Ex.* Земно́й, terrestrial, земляно́й, earthern, (*from* земли́); земляни́стый, earthy; золото́й, golden, золоти́стый, auriferous, (*from* зо́лото).

§ 69. The following is the table of the declensions of nouns adjective with full terminations :—

*Singular Number.*

| Cases. | | Masc. Gender. | Fem. Gender. | Neuter Gender. |
|---|---|---|---|---|
| N. & V. | И. З. | ый, ой, ій, нїй. | ая, яя. | ое, ее. |
| G. | Р. | аго, яго. | ой, ей. | аго, яго. |
| D. | Д. | ому, ему. | ой, ей. | ому, ему. |
| A. | В. | { аго, яго. <br> { ый, ой, ій, нїй. } | ую, юю. | { аго, яго. <br> { ое, ее. } |
| I. | Т. | ымъ, имъ. | ою, ой, ею, ей. | ымъ, имъ. |
| P. | П. | омъ, емъ. | ей. | омъ, емъ. |

*Plural Number.*

| Cases. | | Masc. Gender. | Fem. Gender. | Neuter Gender. |
|---|---|---|---|---|
| N. & V. | И. З. | ые, іе. | ыя, ія. | ыя, ія. |
| G. | Р. | ыхъ, ихъ. | ыхъ, ихъ. | ыхъ, ихъ. |
| D. | Д. | ымъ, имъ. | ымъ, имъ. | ымъ, имъ. |
| A. | В. | { ыхъ, ихъ <br> { ые, іе. } | { ыхъ, ихъ. <br> { ыя, ія. } | ые, ія. |
| I. | Т. | ыми, ими. | ыми, ими. | ыми, ими. |
| P. | П. | ыхъ, ихъ. | ыхъ, ихъ. | ыхъ, ихъ. |

( 32 )

## EXAMPLES OF THE DECLENSION OF NOUNS ADJECTIVE.

### With an Animate Object of the Masculine Gender.

| Cases. | Singular Number. | Plural Number. |
|---|---|---|
| И. З.. N. & V. | сильный орёлъ, powerful eagle. | сильные орлы, powerful eagles. |
| Р. G. | сильнаго орла, of a powerful eagle. | сильныхъ орловъ, of powerful eagles. |
| Д. D. | сильному орлу, to a powerful eagle. | сильнымъ орламъ, to powerful eagles. |
| В. A. | сильнаго орла, powerful eagle. | сильныхъ орловъ, powerful eagles. |
| Т. I. | сильнымъ орломъ, by a powerful eagle. | сильными орлами, by powerful eagles. |
| П. P. | о сильномъ орлѣ, about a powerful eagle. | о сильныхъ орлахъ, about powerful eagles. |

### With an Inanimate Object of the Feminine Gender.

| Cases. | Singular Number. | Plural Number. |
|---|---|---|
| И. З. N. & V. | русская изба, Russian hut. | русскія избы, Russian huts. |
| Р. G. | русской избы, of a Russian hut. | русскихъ избъ, of Russian huts. |
| Д. D. | русской избѣ, to a Russian hut. | русскимъ избамъ, to Russian huts. |
| В. A. | русскую избу, Russian hut. | русскія избы, Russian huts. |
| Т. I. | русскою избою, with a Russian hut. | русскими избами, with Russian huts. |
| П. P. | о, въ русской избѣ, about in a Russian hut. | о, въ русскихъ избахъ, about in Russian huts. |

### With an Inanimate Object of the Neuter Gender.

| Cases. | Singular Number. | Plural Number. |
|---|---|---|
| И. З. N. & V. | прежнее мѣсто, former place. | прежнія мѣста, former places. |
| Р. G. | прежняго мѣста, of a former place. | прежнихъ мѣстъ, of former places. |
| Д. D. | прежнему мѣсту, to a former place. | прежнимъ мѣстамъ, to former places. |
| В. A. | прежнее мѣсто, former place. | прежнія мѣста, former places. |
| Т. I. | прежнимъ мѣстомъ, by a former place. | прежними мѣстами, by former places. |
| П. P. | на прежнемъ мѣстѣ, on a former place. | на прежнихъ мѣстахъ, on former places. |

### With an Animate Object of the Masculine Gender.

| Cases. | Singular Number. | Plural Number. |
|---|---|---|
| N. З.<br>N. & V. | до́брый братъ,<br>kind brother. | до́брые бра́тья,<br>kind brothers. |
| Р.<br>G. | до́браго бра́та,<br>of a kind brother. | до́брыхъ бра́тьевъ,<br>of kind brothers. |
| Д.<br>D. | до́брому бра́ту,<br>to a kind brother. | до́брымъ бра́тьямъ,<br>to kind brothers. |
| В.<br>A. | до́браго бра́та,<br>kind brother. | до́брыхъ бра́тьевъ,<br>kind brothers. |
| Т.<br>I. | до́брымъ бра́томъ,<br>by a kind brother. | до́брыми бра́тьями,<br>by kind brothers. |
| П.<br>P. | о до́бромъ бра́тѣ,<br>about a kind brother. | о до́брыхъ бра́тьяхъ,<br>about kind brothers. |

### With an Animate Object of the Feminine Gender.

| Cases. | Singular Number. | Plural Number. |
|---|---|---|
| Н. З<br>N. & V. | до́брая сестра́,<br>a kind sister. | до́брыя сёстры,<br>kind sisters. |
| Р.<br>G. | до́брой сестры́,<br>of a kind sister. | до́брыхъ сестёръ,<br>of kind sisters. |
| Д.<br>D. | до́брой сестрѣ,<br>to a kind sister. | до́брымъ сестра́мъ,<br>to kind sisters. |
| В.<br>A. | до́брую сестру́,<br>kind sister. | до́брыхъ сестёръ,<br>kind sisters. |
| Т.<br>I. | до́брою сестро́ю,<br>by a kind sister. | до́брыми сестра́ми,<br>by kind sisters. |
| П.<br>P. | о до́брой сестрѣ,<br>about a kind sister. | о до́брыхъ сёстрахъ,<br>about kind sisters. |

### With an Inanimate Object of the Neuter Gender.

| Cases. | Singular Number. | Plural Number. |
|---|---|---|
| Н. З.<br>N. & V. | до́брое дѣ́ло,<br>kind deed. | до́брыя дѣла́,<br>kind deeds. |
| Р.<br>G. | до́браго дѣ́ла,<br>of a kind deed. | до́брыхъ дѣлъ,<br>of kind deeds. |
| Д.<br>D. | до́брому дѣ́лу,<br>to a kind deed. | до́брымъ дѣла́мъ,<br>to kind deeds. |
| В.<br>A. | до́брое дѣ́ло,<br>kind deed. | до́брыя дѣла́,<br>kind deeds. |
| Т.<br>I. | до́брымъ дѣ́ломъ,<br>by a kind deed. | до́брыми дѣла́ми,<br>by kind deeds. |
| П.<br>P. | о до́бромъ дѣ́лѣ,<br>about a kind deed. | о до́брыхъ дѣла́хъ,<br>about kind deeds. |

### With an Inanimate Object of the Masculine Gender.

| Cases. | Singular Number. | Plural Number. |
|---|---|---|
| И. З.<br>N & V. | простой камень,<br>ordinary stone. | простые камни,<br>ordinary stones. |
| Р.<br>G. | простаго камня,<br>of ordinary stone. | простыхъ камней,<br>of ordinary stones. |
| Д.<br>D. | простому камню,<br>to ordinary stone. | простымъ камнямъ,<br>to ordinary stones. |
| В.<br>A. | простой камень,<br>ordinary stone. | простые камни,<br>ordinary stones. |
| Т.<br>I. | простымъ камнемъ,<br>by ordinary stone. | простыми камнями,<br>by ordinary stones. |
| П.<br>P. | о простомъ камнѣ,<br>about ordinary stone. | о простыхъ камняхъ,<br>about ordinary stones. |

### With an Inanimate Object of the Feminine Gender.

| Cases. | Singular Number. | Plural Number. |
|---|---|---|
| И. З.<br>N & V. | простая кость,<br>common bone. | простыя кости,<br>common bones. |
| Р.<br>G. | простой кости,<br>of common bone. | простыхъ костей,<br>of common bones. |
| Д.<br>D. | простой кости,<br>to common bone. | простымъ костямъ,<br>to common bones. |
| В.<br>A. | простую кость,<br>common bone. | простыя кости,<br>common bones. |
| Т.<br>I. | простою костью,<br>by common bone. | простыми костями,<br>by common bones. |
| П.<br>P. | о простой кости,<br>about common bone. | о простыхъ костяхъ,<br>about common bones. |

### With an Inanimate Object of the Neuter Gender.

| Cases. | Singular Number. | Plural Number. |
|---|---|---|
| И. З.<br>N. & V. | простое растѣніе,<br>a common plant. | простыя растѣнія,<br>common plants. |
| Р.<br>G. | простаго растѣнія,<br>of a common plant. | простыхъ растѣній,<br>of common plants. |
| Д.<br>D. | простому растѣнію,<br>to a common plant. | простымъ растѣніямъ,<br>to common plants. |
| В.<br>A. | простое растѣніе,<br>a common plant. | простыя растѣнія,<br>common plants. |
| Т.<br>I. | простымъ растѣніемъ,<br>by a common plant. | простыми растѣніями,<br>by common plants. |
| П.<br>P. | о простомъ растѣніи,<br>about a common plant. | о простыхъ растѣніяхъ,<br>about common plants. |

## With an Inanimate Object of the Masculine Gender.

| Cases. | Singular Number. | Plural Number. |
|---|---|---|
| И. З.<br>N. & V. | лѣтній день,<br>summer day. | лѣтніе дни,<br>summer days. |
| Р.<br>G. | лѣтняго дня,<br>of a summer day. | лѣтнихъ дней,<br>of summer days. |
| Д.<br>D. | лѣтнему дню,<br>to a summer day. | лѣтнимъ днямъ,<br>to summer days. |
| В.<br>A. | лѣтній день,<br>summer day. | лѣтніе дни,<br>summer days. |
| Т.<br>I. | лѣтнимъ днёмъ,<br>by a summer day. | лѣтними днями,<br>by summer days. |
| П.<br>P. | о лѣтнемъ днѣ,<br>about a summer day. | о лѣтнихъ дняхъ,<br>about summer days. |

## With an Inanimate Object of the Feminine Gender.

| Cases. | Singular Number. | Plural Number. |
|---|---|---|
| И. З.<br>N. & V. | лѣтняя ночь,<br>summer night. | лѣтнія ночи,<br>summer nights. |
| Р.<br>G. | лѣтней ночи,<br>of a summer night. | лѣтнихъ ночей,<br>of summer nights. |
| Д.<br>D. | лѣтней ночи,<br>to a summer night. | лѣтнимъ ночамъ,<br>to summer nights. |
| В.<br>A. | лѣтнюю ночь,<br>summer night. | лѣтнія ночи,<br>summer nights. |
| Т.<br>I. | лѣтнею ночью,<br>by a summer night. | лѣтними ночами,<br>by summer nights. |
| П.<br>P. | о лѣтней ночи,<br>about a summer night. | о лѣтнихъ ночахъ,<br>about summer nights. |

## With an Inanimate Object of the Neuter Gender.

| Cases. | Singular Number. | Plural Number. |
|---|---|---|
| И. З.<br>N. & V. | лѣтнее одѣяло,<br>summer coverlet. | лѣтнія одѣяла,<br>summer coverlets. |
| Р.<br>G. | лѣтняго одѣяла,<br>of a summer coverlet. | лѣтнихъ одѣялъ,<br>of summer coverlets. |
| Д.<br>D. | лѣтнему одѣялу,<br>to a summer covelet. | лѣтнимъ одѣяламъ,<br>to summer coverlets. |
| В.<br>A. | лѣтнее одѣяло,<br>summer coverlet. | лѣтнія одѣяла,<br>summer coverlets. |
| Т.<br>I. | лѣтнимъ одѣяломъ,<br>with a summer coverlet. | лѣтними одѣялами,<br>with summer coverlets. |
| П.<br>P. | о лѣтнемъ одѣялѣ,<br>about a summer coverlet. | о лѣтнихъ одѣялахъ,<br>about summer coverlets. |

( 36 )

§ 70. Certain Possessive Adjectives which are derived from animate objects, and which terminate in *ій, ья, ье,* such as оле́н*ій* *-ья -ье*, of a deer, are declined in the following manner:—

*Singular Number.*

| Cases. | | Masc. Termination. | Fem. Termination. | Neuter Termination. |
|---|---|---|---|---|
| N.&V. | И. З. | оле́нiй. | оле́нья. | оле́нье. |
| G. | Р. | оле́ньяго. | оле́ньяго. | оле́ньяго. |
| D. | Д. | оле́ньему. | оле́ньему. | оле́ньему. |
| A. | В. | оле́нiй. | оле́нью. | оле́нье. |
| I. | Т. | оле́ньимъ. | оле́ньею. | оле́ньимъ. |
| P. | П. | объ оле́ньемъ. | объ оле́ньей. | объ оле́ньемъ. |

Belonging to a deer.

*Plural Number.*

| Cases. | | Masc. Termination. | Fem. Termination. | Neuter Termination. |
|---|---|---|---|---|
| N.&V. | И. З. | оле́ньи. | оле́ньи. | оле́ньи. |
| G. | Р. | оле́нихъ. | оле́ньихъ. | оле́ньихъ. |
| D. | Д. | оле́ньи. | оле́ньимъ. | оле́ньимъ. |
| A. | В. | оле́ньи. | оле́ньи. | оле́ньи. |
| I. | Т. | оле́ньими. | оле́ньими. | оле́ньими. |
| P. | П. | объ оле́ньихъ. | объ оле́ньихъ. | объ оле́ньихъ. |

§ 71. The Possessive Adjective Бо́жій, Divine, is declined as below.

| Cases. | | *Singular Number.* | | | *Plural Number.* |
|---|---|---|---|---|---|
| | | Masculine. | Feminine. | Neuter. | All Genders |
| N.&V. | И. З. | Бо́жій. | Бо́жія. | Бо́жіе. | Бо́жіи. |
| G. | Р. | Бо́жія. | Бо́жіей. | Бо́жія. | Бо́жіихъ. |
| D. | Д. | Бо́жію. | Бо́жіей. | Бо́жію. | Бо́жіимъ. |
| A. | В. | Бо́жій. | Бо́жію. | Бо́жіе. | Бо́жіи. |
| I. | Т. | Бо́жіимъ. | Бо́жіею. | Бо́жіимъ. | Бо́жіими. |
| P. | П. | О Бо́жіемъ. | О Бо́жіей. | О Бо́жіемъ. | О Бо́жіихъ. |

§ 72. The following is a table showing the several forms of the shortened terminations of possessive nouns adjective:—

( 37 )

| Cases. | | Singular Number. | | | Plural Number. |
|---|---|---|---|---|---|
| | | Masculine. | Feminine. | Neuter. | All Genders. |
| N. & V. | И. З. | ъ, ь, | а, я, | о, е, | ы, и. |
| G. | Р. | а, я, | ой, ей, | а, я, | ыхъ, ихъ. |
| D. | Д. | у, ю, | ой, ей, | у, ю, | ымъ, имъ. |
| A. | В. | { а, я, <br> { ъ, ь, } | у, ю, | о, е, | { ыхъ, ихъ, <br> { ы, и. } |
| I. | Т. | ымъ, имъ, | ою, ею, | ымъ, имъ, | ыми, ями. |
| P. | П. | омъ, емъ, | ой, ей, | омъ, емъ, | ыхъ, ихъ. |

*Examples of the declensions of Nouns Adjective with shortened terminations. Possessive adjectives derived from personal nouns* (vide § 58, N°. 2).

*Singular Number.*

| Cases. | | Masculine Gender. | Feminine Gender. | Neuter Gender. |
|---|---|---|---|---|
| N. & V. | И. З. | отцо́въ, | бра́тнина, | сёстрино. |
| G. | Р. | отцо́ва, | бра́тниной, | сёстрина. |
| D. | Д. | отцо́ву, | бра́тниной, | сёстрину. |
| A. | В. | { отцо́ва, <br> { отцо́въ, } | бра́тнину, | сёстрино. |
| I. | Т. | отцо́вымъ, | бра́тниною, | сёстринымъ. |
| P. | П. | объ отцо́вомъ, | о бра́тниной, | о сёстриномъ. |
| | | Of the father. | Of the brother. | Of the sister. |

*Plural Number.*

| Cases. | | Masculine Gender. | Feminine Gender. | Neuter Gender. |
|---|---|---|---|---|
| N. & V. | И. З. | отцо́вы, | бра́тнины, | сёстрины. |
| G. | Р. | отцо́выхъ, | бра́тниныхъ, | сёстриныхъ. |
| D. | Д. | отцо́вымъ, | бра́тнинымъ, | сёстринымъ. |
| A. | В. | { отцо́выхъ, <br> { отцо́вы, } | { бра́тниныхъ, <br> { бра́тнины, } | { сёстриныхъ, <br> { сёстрины. } |
| I. | Т. | отцо́выми, | бра́тниными, | сёстриными. |
| P. | П. | объ отцо́выхъ, | о бра́тниныхъ, | о сёстриныхъ. |

*Singular Number.*

| Cases. | | Masculine Gender. | Feminine Gender. | Neuter Gender. |
|---|---|---|---|---|
| N. & V. | И. З. | Нико́линъ день, | Екатери́нина да́ча, | Цари́цыно село́. |
| G. | Р. | Нико́лина дня, | Екатери́ниной да́чи, | Цари́цына села́. |
| D. | Д. | Нико́лину дню, | Екатери́ниной да́чѣ, | Цари́цыну селу́. |
| A. | В. | Нико́линъ день, | Екатери́нину да́чу, | Цари́цыно село́. |
| I. | Т. | Нико́линымъ днёмъ, | Екатери́ниною да́чею, | Цари́цынымъ село́мъ. |
| P. | П. | О Нико́линомъ днѣ, | въ Екатери́ниной да́чѣ, | о Цари́цыномъ селѣ. |
| | | St. Nicholas's day. | Catherine's country-house. | Tsarína's [1] village. |

---

[1] Title of the Russian Empress. *Trans.*

The plural of the three last examples is according to those given in the table above.

*Obs.*—Qualifying nouns adjective with shortened terminations are inflected only in poetry,

*Ex.* Тамъ бушу́етъ[1] сѝне мо́ре
There rages the blue sea.

Я дойду́[2] до си́ня мо́ря
I will go to the blue sea.

Подивлю́ся[3] си́пю мо́рю
I will admire the blue sea.

Погляжу́[4] на си́пе мо́ре
I will gaze on the blue sea.

§ 73. It is especially necessary to observe the following rules for nouns adjective :—

(1) To insure the agreement of nouns adjective with nouns substantive in gender, number and case, the nominative case, plural, of the adjective in question must, if the substantive is of the masculine gender, always terminate in *е*. Similarly, if the substantive is of the feminine or neuter gender, the nominative case, plural, of the adjective will terminate in *я*. *Ex.* Хра́брые во́ины brave warriors, from во́инъ; бѣ́лыя стѣ́ны white walls, from стѣна́; си́ния стёкла blue glasses, from стекло́.

(2) With regard to the adjective Бо́жій Divine, the nominative case, plural, terminates (for all genders) in *и*. *Ex.* Бо́жіи Хра́мы God's temples, from храмъ; Бо́жіи Це́ркви God's churches, from це́рковь; Бо́жіи Созда́нія God's creatures, from созда́ніе.

(3) Adjectives derived from animate nouns, and which terminate in *ій*, have in the nominative case of the plural number *ьи* (for all genders). *Ex.* Оле́ньи рога́, horns of a deer; медвѣ́жьи шу́бы, bearskin coats; пти́чьи гнѣзда́, birds' nests.

(4) Nouns adjective of the *masculine* gender terminate in *ой* only when the accent lies on the ante-penultimate letter. *Ex.* худо́й bad, нѣмо́й dumb, &c. When the accent is *not* on the ante-penultimate letter or syllable, adjectives of the masculine gender terminate in *ый* or *ій*. *Ex.* до́брый kind, вели́кій great, &c.

---

[1] Present tense of бушева́ть. *Trans.*
[2] Future tense of дойти́. *Trans.*
[3] Future tense of подиви́ться *Trans.*
[4] Future tense of погляде́ть. *Trans.*

(5) Nouns adjective which terminate in *ній* have in the genitive case, singular, the termination *яго*, and are declined according to the table of nouns adjective terminating in *ній* (*Vide* § 69). *Ex.* синій blue, &c. All other nouns adjective ending in *ій* have in the following cases of the singular number the termination here specified:—In the genitive case *аго*, in the dative *ому*, in the instrumental *имъ*, in the prepositional *омъ*. In the plural number, however, they are declined like adjectives which terminate in *ній*. The following is an instance of this rule:—высокій high, &c.

## The Noun of Number or Numeral.
(имя числительное).

§ 74. The numerals indicate the quantity or number of the objects spoken of. *Ex.* одинъ one, первый first, дюжина dozen, &c.

§ 75. Numerals are divided into—

(1) *Cardinal* (количественное), or those which point out the number of the objects, by answering to the question Сколько? How many? *Ans.* Одинъ one, два two, &c.

(2) *Ordinal* (порядковое), or those which determine the sequence or order in which one object shall follow another. The ordinals answer to the question Который? Which? *Ans.* Первый first, &c.

### Table of the Russian Numerals.

| Cardinal. | | | Ordinal. | | |
|---|---|---|---|---|---|
| одинъ, *masc.* | } *sing.* | | первый, *masc.* | } *sing.* | |
| одна, *fem.* | | | ——ая, *fem.* | | |
| одно, *neut.* | | 1 | ——ое, *neut.* | | 1st. |
| одни, *masc. & neut.* | } *plur.* | | ——ые, *masc.* | } *plur.* | |
| одне, *fem.* | | | ——ыя, *fem. & neut.* | | |
| два, *sing., for all gen.* | } | 2 | второй -ая -ое, *sing.* | } | 2nd. |
| двѣ, *plur.*, „ „ | | | ——ые -ыя, *plur.* | | |
| три, | | 3 | третій -ья -ье -ьи, | | 3rd. |
| четыре, | | 4 | четвёртый -ая -ое -ые -ыя, | | 4th. |
| пять, | | 5 | пятый, &c. | | 5th. |
| шесть, | | 6 | шестой, &c. | | 6th. |
| семь, | | 7 | седьмой, &c. | | 7th. |
| восемь, | | 8 | восьмой, &c. | | 8th. |
| девять, | | 9 | девятый, &c. | | 9th. |
| десять, | | 10 | десятый, &c. | | 10th. |
| одиннадцать, | | 11 | одиннадцатый, &c. | | 11th. |
| двѣнадцать, | | 12 | двѣнадцатый, &c. | | 12th. |

| Cardinal Numbers (continued). | | | Ordinal Numbers (continued). | |
|---|---|---|---|---|
| трипа́дцать, | 13 | | трипа́дцатый, &c. | 13th. |
| четы́рпадцать, | 14 | | четы́рпадцатый, &c. | 14th. |
| пятна́дцать, | 15 | | пятна́дцатый, &c. | 15th. |
| шестна́дцать, | 16 | | шестна́дцатый, &c. | 16th. |
| семна́дцать, | 17 | | семна́дцатый, &c. | 17th. |
| восемна́дцать, | 18 | | восьмна́дцатый, &c. | 18th. |
| девятна́дцать, | 19 | | девятна́дцатый, &c. | 19th. |
| два́дцать, | 20 | | двадца́тый, &c. | 20th. |
| два́дцать-оди́нъ, &c. | 21, &c. | | два́дцать-пе́рвый, &c. | 21st, &c. |
| три́дцать, | 30 | | тридца́тый, | 30th. |
| | | | три́дцать-пе́рвый, &c. | 31st, &c. |
| со́рокъ, | 40 | | сороково́й, &c. | 40th. |
| | | | со́рокъ-пе́рвый, &c. | 41st, &c. |
| пятьдеся́тъ, | 50 | | пятидеся́тый, | 50th. |
| | | | пятьдеся́тъ-пе́рвый, &c. | 51st, &c. |
| шестьдеся́тъ, | 60 | | шестидеся́тый, &c. | 60th. |
| | | | шестьдеся́тъ-пе́рвый, &c. | 61st, &c. |
| се́мьдесятъ, | 70 | | семидеся́тый, | 70th. |
| | | | се́мьдесятъ-пе́рвый, &c. | 71st, &c. |
| во́семьдесятъ, | 80 | | восьмидеся́тый, &c. | 80th. |
| | | | во́семьдесятъ-пе́рвый, &c. | 81st, &c. |
| девяно́сто, | 90 | | девяно́стый, &c. | 90th. |
| | | | девяно́сто-пе́рвый, &c. | 91st, &c. |
| сто, | 100 | | со́тый, &c. | 100th. |
| | | | сто-пе́рвый, &c. | 101st, &c. |
| две́сти, | 200 | | двухъ-со́тый, &c. | 200th. |
| | | | две́сти-пе́рвый, &c. | 201st, &c. |
| три́ста, | 300 | | трёхъ-со́тый, &c. | 300th. |
| | | | три́ста-пе́рвый, &c. | 301st, &c. |
| четы́реста, | 400 | | четырёхъ-со́тый, &c. | 400th. |
| | | | четы́реста-пе́рвый, &c. | 401st, &c. |
| пятьсо́тъ, | 500 | | пяти-со́тый, &c. | 500th. |
| | | | пятьсо́тъ-пе́рвый, &c. | 501st, &c. |
| шестьсо́тъ, | 600 | | шести-со́тый, &c. | 600th. |
| | | | шестьсо́тъ пе́рвый, &c. | 601st, &c. |
| семьсо́тъ, | 700 | | семи-со́тый, &c. | 700th. |
| | | | семьсо́тъ пе́рвый, &c. | 701st, &c. |
| восемьсо́тъ, | 800 | | восьми-со́тый, &c. | 800th. |
| | | | восемьсо́тъ пе́рвый, &c. | 801st, &c. |
| девятьсо́тъ, | 900 | | девяти-со́тый, &c. | 900th. |
| | | | девятьсо́тъ пе́рвый, &c. | 901st, &c. |
| ты́сяча, | 1000 | | ты́сячный, &c. | 1000th, &c. |
| двѣ ты́сячи, | 2000 | | двухъ-ты́сячный, &c. | 2000th, &c. |
| де́сять ты́сячъ, | 10,000 | | десяти-ты́сячный, &c. | 10,000th, &c. |
| сто ты́сячъ, | 100,000 | | сто-ты́сячный, &c. | 100,000th, &c. |
| милліо́нъ, | 1,000,000 | | милліо́нный, &c. | 1000,000th, &c. |
| два милліо́на, | 2,000,000 | | двухъ-милліо́нный, &c. | 2000,000th, &c. |
| ты́сяча милліо́новъ, | 1000,000,000 | | ты́сяче милліо́нный, | 1000,000,000th, &c. |
| (т. е. миліа́рдъ) | (i. e. milliard) | | | |
| билліо́нъ, | 1,000,000,000 | | билліо́нный, &c. | 1,000,000,000th, &c. |

| *Fractional Numerals.* | | | *Circumstantial Numerals.* | |
|---|---|---|---|---|
| половина, | ½ | | другой, | other. |
| треть, | ⅓ | | последній, | last. |
| четверть, | ¼ | | *Proportional Numerals.* | |
| осьмуха *or* осьмушка, | ⅛ | | двойной, | double. |
| полтора, | 1½ | | тройной, | treble. |
| полтретья, | 2½ | | четверной, | quadruple. |
| полчетверта, | 3½ | | стократный *or* сторачный, | centuple. |

*Collective Numerals.*

| | | | | |
|---|---|---|---|---|
| двое, | трое, | четверо, | патеро, | тройка three, пяток five, десяток |
| шестеро, | десятеро. | | | ten, дюжина dozen, and пол-дюжины |
| *Sets of Two, &c., &c.* | | | | half dozen; два десятка score, сотна |
| пара pair, оба both, двойка two, | | | | hundred. |

§ 76. To the class of cardinals belong—

(1) *Collective* (собирательное) numerals, such as пара pair, тройка triplet, двое set of two, оба both, дюжина dozen, &c.

(2) *Fractional* (дробное), such as четверть quarter, половина half, полтора one-and-a-half, &c.

§ 77. Numerals, according to their composition, can be either—

(1) *Simple* (простое), or such as are formed from one primary word; for instance, два, три, первый, &c.

(2) *Compound* (сложное), or such as are made up of two or more words: двѣ-надцать (двѣ-на-десять) twelve, пять-десять, fifty; сто-первый, hundred (and) first; &c.

§ 78. The cardinal numerals are declined like nouns substantive, and the ordinal like nouns adjective ending in *ый* and *ой*. Третій third, is declined after the manner of nouns adjective terminating in *ій*, which are derived from animate nouns. (*Vide* § 70).

§ 79. The ordinal numeral первый, when used in the sense of лучшій best, or отличный excellent, has degrees of comparison—первый, первѣйшій, самый первый.

§ 80. The numerals единый sole, двоякій two-fold, тройной ternary, and the like, have the meaning of qualifying nouns adjective, and are declined as nouns adjective.

§ 81. The declension of the cardinal numerals is as follows :—

*Singular Number.*  *Plural Number.*

| Cases. | | Masc. | Fem. | Neut. | Masc. & Neut. | Fem. |
|---|---|---|---|---|---|---|
| N. | И. | одинъ, | одна́, | одно́. | одни́, | одне́. |
| G. | Р. | одного́, | одно́й, | одного́. | одни́хъ, | одне́хъ. |
| D. | Д. | одному́, | одно́й, | одному́. | одни́мъ, | одне́мъ. |
| A. | В. | {одного́ / одинъ} | одну́, | одно́. | {одни́хъ, / одни́,} | {одне́хъ. / одне́.} |
| I. | Т. | одни́мъ, | одно́ю, | одни́мъ. | одни́ми, | одне́ми. |
| P. | П. | объ одно́мъ, | объ одно́й, | объ одно́мъ. | объ одни́хъ, | объ одне́хъ. |

one.

| Cases. | | Masc. & Neut. | Fem. | All Genders. | |
|---|---|---|---|---|---|
| N. | И. | два, | две́. | три, | четы́ре. |
| G. | Р. | двухъ, | двухъ. | трёхъ, | четырёхъ. |
| D. | Д. | двумъ, | двумъ. | трёмъ, | четырёмъ. |
| A. | В. | {двухъ, / два,} | {двухъ. / две́.} | {трёхъ, / три,} | {четырёхъ. / четы́ре.} |
| I. | Т. | двумя́, | двумя́. | тремя́, | четырьмя́. |
| P. | П. | о двухъ, | о двухъ. | о трёхъ, | о четырёхъ. |

two. three. four.

| Cases. | | All Genders. | All Genders. | All Genders. | All Genders. |
|---|---|---|---|---|---|
| N. | И. | пять. | во́семь. | оди́ннадцать. | со́рокъ. |
| G. | Р. | пяти́. | осьми́. | оди́ннадцати. | сорока́. |
| D. | Д. | пяти́. | осьми́. | оди́ннадцати. | сорока́. |
| A. | В. | пять. | во́семь. | оди́ннадцать. | со́рокъ. |
| I. | Т. | пятью́. | осемью́. | оди́ннадцатью. | сорока́. |
| P. | П. | о пяти́. | о восьми́. | при оди́ннадцати. | о сорока́. |

five. eight. eleven. forty.

| Cases. | | All Genders. | All Genders. | All Genders. | All Genders. |
|---|---|---|---|---|---|
| N. | И. | пятьдеся́тъ. | сто. | две́сти. | пять-со́тъ. |
| G. | Р. | пяти́десяти. | ста. | двухъ-со́тъ. | пяти-со́тъ. |
| D. | Д | пяти́десяти. | сту, ста. | двумъ-ста́мъ. | пяти-ста́мъ. |
| A. | В. | пятьдеся́тъ. | сто. | две́сти. | пять-со́тъ. |
| I. | Т. | пятью́десятью. | ста. | двумя́-ста́ми. | пятью-ста́ми. |
| P. | П. | о пяти́десяти. | о ста. | въ двухъ-стахъ. | о пяти-стахъ. |

fifty. a hundred. two hundred. five hundred.

|  | | Singular Number. | Plural Number. |
|---|---|---|---|
| Cases. | | All Genders. | All Genders. |
| N. | И. | ты́сяча, | ты́сячи. |
| G. | Р. | ты́сячи, | ты́сячъ. |
| D. | Д. | ты́сячѣ, | ты́сячамъ. |
| A. | В. | ты́сячу, | ты́сячи. |
| I. | Т. | ты́сячею, | ты́сячами. |
| P. | П. | о ты́сячѣ, | о ты́сячахъ. |

thousand.

*Note.*—When before the genitive, dative, and prepositional cases of *восемь*, prepositions terminating with a vowel are used, in place of *осьми* it is usual to write *восьми*. *Ex.* ·*у восьми ученикóвъ*, *with* eight pupils; *для восьми солдáтъ*, *for* eight soldiers; *о восьми книгахъ*, *about* eight books.

*Obs.*—The dative case of the numerals *сорокъ* and *сто*, when used with the preposition *по* up to, terminates in *у*, and not in *а*. *Ex.* Имъ дáли *по сту* рублéй, They gave them 100 roubles *each*.

§ 82. Шесть (6), семь (7), дéвять (9), and дéсять (10), are declined like пять (5); двѣнáдцать (12), тринáдцать (13), четырнадцать (14), пятнáдцать (15), шестнáдцать (16), семнáдцать (17), восемнáдцать (18), девятнáдцать (19), двáдцать (20) and трúдцать (30), like одúнадцать (11); шестьдесятъ (60), and семьдесятъ (70), like пятьдесятъ (50); восемьдесятъ (80), like восемь (8) and дéсять (10) joined together; девяносто (90), like сто (100); трúста (300), and четы́реста (400), like двѣсти (200); шестьсотъ (600), семьсотъ (700), восемьсотъ (800), and девятьсотъ (900), like пятьсотъ (500).

§ 83. With regard to the declension of the cardinal numerals, it must be observed that, in the instances of одúнъ, два, три, четы́ре, the accusative case is like the nominative or the genitive, according to whether the noun defined by the numeral in question is animate or inanimate. In the instances, however, of the rest of the cardinal numerals commencing with пять five, the accusative case is like the nominative, without distinction as to the nouns being animate or inanimate.

§ 84. *Examples of the Declension of the Collective and Fractional Numerals.*

| Cases. | Masc. & Neut. | Fem. | For all Genders. | |
|---|---|---|---|---|
| N. Н. | о́ба, | о́бѣ. | тро́е. | че́тверо. |
| G. Р. | обо́ихъ, | обѣ́ихъ. | тро́ихъ. | четверы́хъ. |
| D. Д. | обо́имъ, | обѣ́имъ. | тро́имъ. | четверы́мъ. |
| A. В. | { обо́ихъ, / о́ба, | обѣ́ихъ. / о́бѣ. | тро́ихъ. / тро́е. | четверы́хъ. / че́тверо. |
| I. Т. | обо́ими, | обѣ́ими. | тро́ими. | четверы́ми. |
| P. П. | въ обо́ихъ, | при обѣ́ихъ. | о тро́ихъ. | на четверы́хъ. |
|  | both. | | set of three. | set of four. |

Дво́е set of two, and о́бое both, are declined like тро́е; пя́теро set of five, ше́стеро set of six, &c., are declined like че́тверо.

| Cases. | Masc. and Neut. | Fem. | All Genders. |
|---|---|---|---|
| N. П. | полтора́, | полторы́, | полтора́ста. |
| G. Р. | полу́тора, | полу́торы, | полу́тораста. |
| D. Д. | полу́тору, | полу́торѣ, | полу́торасту. |
| A. В. | полтора́, | полторы́, | полтора́ста. |
| I. Т. | полу́торымъ, | полу́торою, | полу́тораста. |
| P. П. | о полу́торѣ, | въ полу́торѣ, | о полу́торастѣ. |
|  | one and a half. | | one hundred and fifty. |

§ 85. In the instances of the compound cardinal numerals, every word is declined, together with the substantive and adjective with which they may be joined:—

| | | | |
|---|---|---|---|
| N. Н. | три́ста солда́тъ. | | семьсо́тъ но́выхъ кни́гъ. |
| G. Р. | трёхъ сотъ солда́тъ. | | семисо́тъ но́выхъ кни́гъ. |
| D. Д. | трёмъ стамъ солда́тамъ. | | семиста́мъ но́вымъ кни́гамъ. |
| A. В. | три́ста солда́тъ. | | семьсо́тъ но́выхъ кни́гъ. |
| I. Т. | тремя́ стами́ солда́тами | | семьюста́ми но́выми кни́гами. |
| P. П. | о трёхъ стахъ солда́тахъ. | | о семиста́хъ но́выхъ кни́гахъ. |
| | three hundred soldiers. | | seven hundred new books. |

| | |
|---|---|
| N. П. | четы́реста два́дцать оди́нъ рубль. |
| G. Р. | четырёхъсотъ двадцати́ одного́ рубля́. |
| D. Д. | четырёмъстамъ двадцати́ одному́ рублю́. |
| A. В. | четы́реста два́дцать оди́нъ рубль. |
| I. Т. | четырьмяста́ми двадцатью́ одни́мъ рублёмъ. |
| P. П. | о четырёхъстахъ двадцати́ одно́мъ рублѣ́. |
| | four hundred and twenty-one roubles. |

| | | |
|---|---|---|
| N. | И. | тысяча восемь сотъ тридцать шесть рублей, |
| G. | Р. | тысячи осьми сотъ тридцати шести рублей, |
| D. | Д. | тысячѣ осьми стамъ тридцати шести рублямъ, |
| A. | В. | тысячу восемь сотъ тридцать шесть рублей, |
| I. | Т. | тысячею восемью стами тридцатью шестью рублями, |
| P. | П. | о тысячѣ осьми стахъ тридцати шести рубляхъ, |

one thousand eight hundred and thirty-six roubles.

§ 86. The last word of the compound ordinal numerals is alone declined with the substantive and the adjective joined thereto.

| Ex. | N. | И. | тысяча восемь сотъ тридцать шестой годъ. |
|---|---|---|---|
| | G. | Р. | „ „ „ „ шестаго года. |
| | D. | Д. | „ „ „ „ шестому году. |
| | A. | В. | „ „ „ „ шестой годъ. |
| | I. | Т. | „ „ „ „ шестымъ годомъ. |
| | P. | П. | о „ „ „ „ шестомъ годѣ. |

the one thousand eight hundred and thirty-sixth year.

§ 87. Ordinal numerals, like nouns adjective, terminate in *ой* only when the accent falls on the ante-penultimate letter. *Ex.* второ́й, second; шесто́й, sixth; восьмо́й, eighth; &c.

§ 88. When the *collective* and *fractional* numerals are declined with nouns substantive, the numeral in question is alone subject to inflection, the substantive remaining in the *genitive* case.

| Ex. | N. | И. | десятокъ грушъ, | пара лошадей, | четверть листа. |
|---|---|---|---|---|---|
| | G. | Р. | десятка грушъ, | пары лошадей, | четверти листа. |
| | D. | Д. | десятку грушъ, | парѣ лошадей, | четверти листа. |
| | A. | В. | десятокъ грушъ, | пару лошадей, | четверть листа. |
| | I. | Т. | десяткомъ грушъ, | парою лошадей, | четвертью листа. |
| | P. | П. | о десяткѣ грушъ, | о парѣ лошадей, | о четверти листа. |
| | | | set of ten pears, from груша. | pair of horses, from лошадь. | leaf of paper, from листъ, &c. |

## THE PRONOUN (Мѣстоимѣнie).

§ 89. The pronoun is used in place of a noun.

§ 90. Pronouns are—

(1) *Personal* (личное): *Ex.* of first person, Я I, мы we; of second person, ты thou, вы you; of third person, онъ he, она́ she, оно́ it; они́ they (*masc.* and *neut. genders*), онѣ they (*fem. gender*). *Ex.* Я пишу́,[1] I am writing; ты о́чень приле́женъ,[2] *thou* (art) very diligent; онъ до́брый това́рищъ, *he* (is) a good comrade; они́ уѣхали,[3] *they* went away.

---

[1] Present tense of писать. *Trans.*   [2] Shortened form of прилѣжный. *Trans.*
[3] Past tense of уѣхать. *Trans.*

(2) *Reflective* (возвра́тное), or those which show that the person or persons, or thing or things, perform an action which is reflected back to the agent or agents. There is in the Russian language but one such pronoun for both numbers and all genders. This is себя́, self. *Ex.* Онъ отка́зываетъ себѣ въ пи́щѣ, *He* denies *himself* food; Ты дово́ленъ собо́ю, *Thou* (art) satisfied with *thyself*; Они́ о себѣ не забо́тятся, *They* do not take care of *themselves*.

(3) *Demonstrative* (указа́тельное), or those which serve to indicate any kind of object; such as, *сей, сія́, сіе́, сіи́,* this, these; *этотъ -а -о -и,* this, these; *тотъ -а -о -ѣ,* that, those; *о́ный -ая -ое -ые -ыя* this one, that one, *or* the said; *тако́й -ая -ое -ые -ыя* such a one, &c. *Ex.* Этотъ домъ краси́въ, а тотъ безобра́зенъ, *This* house (is) pretty, but *that one* (is) ugly.

(4) *Possessive* (притяжа́тельное), or those which denote to which of the three persons an object belongs; such as *мой -я́ -ё -и́,* my, *or* mine; *твой -я́ -ё -и́,* thy *or* thine; *его́,* his *or* its (*lit.* of him *or* of it); *свой -я́ -ё -и́,* his, her, its *or* their own; *нашъ -а -е -и,* our, ours; *вашъ -а -е -и,* your, yours; *ихъ,* their *or* theirs (*lit.* of them). *Ex.* вотъ мо́й столъ, ва́ша кни́га, твое́ перо́, Here (is) *my* table, *your* book, *thy* pen.

(5) *Relative* (относи́тельное), or those which are used in place of nouns, and which form a connection between the person or persons speaking and the object or objects about which they speak; such as, *кото́рый -ая -ое,* who, which, what; *ко́й -оя -ое,* who, which, what; *кто,* who; *что,* what; *чей -ья -ьё -ьи,* whose; *како́й -ая -ое,* what sort of. *Ex.* Я купи́лъ кни́гу кото́рую давно́ жела́лъ имѣ́ть, I have bought a book, *which* I have long wished to have.

(6) *Interrogative* (вопроси́тельное), or those which, in form, are the same as the relative pronouns, and which by means of questions endeavour to ascertain to whom or to what an object belongs. *Ex.* Кото́рый часъ? What o'clock (is it)? Кто пришёлъ? Who has come? Чей домъ? Whose house (is) it?

(7) *Definite* (опредѣли́тельное), or those which point with preciseness to the person or object spoken of; such as, *самъ -а́ -о́ -и;* *са́мый -ая -ое -ые -ыя,* the same, the very same; *весь, вся, всё, всѣ,* the whole, all; *ка́ждый -ая -ое -ые -ыя,* each one, every one. *Ex.* Онъ *самъ* былъ тамъ, He *himself* was there; Я ви́дѣлъ э́ту са́мую кни́гу, I saw this *same* book.

(8) *Indefinite* (неопредѣлённое), or those which speak somewhat uncertainly of a person or thing; such as, *нѣкто*, somebody; *нѣчто*, something; *нѣкоторый -ая -ое -ые -ыя*, someone, a certain one; *никто́*, nobody; *ничто́*, nothing; *кто́*, any one; *кое-что́*, something; *ино́й -а́я -о́е -ы́е -ы́я*, another; *кто́-ли́бо*, somebody or other; *что́ ли́бо*, something or other; *кто́-ни-бу́дь*, somebody or other; *что́-ни-бу́дь*, something or other. *Ex*. Въ нѣкоторомъ городѣ были разли́чныя злоупотребле́нія, In a *certain* city there were abuses of various kinds; Онъ написа́лъ кое-что́ но́вое, He wrote *something* new.

To the class of indefinite pronouns belongs the word нѣско́лькій *-ая -ое -ые -ыя*, some, a few. This word is used, however, only in the oblique cases of the plural number. *Ex*. нѣско́лькихъ, нѣско́лькимъ, нѣско́лькими, о нѣско́лькихъ.

*Obs.*—The pronoun *вся́кій -ая -ое -ые -ыя* every one, all, is a *definite* pronoun when used in the sense of *ка́ждый -ая -ое -ые -ыя*, each one. *Ex*. Вся́кій (или ка́ждый) обя́занъ труди́ться, *Each one* (is) obliged to labour. And it is an *indefinite* pronoun when used in the sense conveyed in the following sentence: Здѣсь роди́тся вся́каго ро́да хлѣбъ, Corn of *every* kind grows here.

The cardinal numeral *оди́нъ*, one, a, an, has sometimes the meaning of an indefinite pronoun. *Ex*. Оди́нъ мой прія́тель отпра́вился въ Ло́ндонъ, A (*certain*) friend of mine has set out for London. In this sentence *оди́нъ* stands for *нѣ́который* or *нѣ́кто*.

§ 91. Some of the pronouns are declined as substantives, and others as adjectives. The pronouns declined as substantives are the following :—the personal, *я, ты, мы, вы, онъ, она́, оно́, они́, онѣ*; the reflective, *себя́*; some of the relative or interrogative, such as *кто, что*; and the indefinite, *никто́, ничто́, нѣ́кто, нѣ́что*. All the others, which have for each gender a special termination, are declined as adjectives.

§ 92. *Declension of the Pronouns.*

(1) Pronouns declined like substantives :—

*Singular Number.*

| Cases. | All Genders. | | Masc. | Fem. | Neut. |
|---|---|---|---|---|---|
| N. И. | я I, | ты thou. | онъ he. | она́ she. | оно́ it. |
| G. Р. | меня́, | тебя́, | его́, | ея́, | его́. |
| D. Д. | мнѣ, | тебѣ, | ему́, | ей, | ему́. |
| A. В. | меня́, | тебя́. | его́, | её, | его́. |
| I. Т. | мною́, | тобою́,, | имъ, | ею, | имъ. |
| P. П. | обо мнѣ | на тебѣ, | о нёмъ, | при ней, | въ нёмъ. |

*Plural Number.*

| Cases. | | All Genders. | Masc. | Fem. | Neut. |
|---|---|---|---|---|---|
| N. | И. | мы we, вы you. | они́ they. | онѣ́ they. | они́ they. |
| G. | Р. | насъ, васъ, | ихъ, | ихъ, | ихъ. |
| D. | Д. | намъ, вамъ, | имъ, | имъ, | имъ. |
| A. | В. | насъ, васъ, | ихъ, | ихъ. | ихъ. |
| I. | Т. | на́ми, ва́ми, | и́ми, | и́ми, | и́ми. |
| P. | П. | о насъ, на васъ, | о нихъ, | о нихъ, | въ нихъ. |

*Obs.*—With regard to the declension of the pronouns of the third person онъ, она́, оно́, они́, онѣ́, it is necessary, when prepositions are used with the oblique cases of such pronouns, to prefix the letter *н* to the case in question; thus, У него́ мо́й ножъ, *He has my knife*; Я иду́ къ нему́, къ ней, съ нимъ съ нею, съ ни́ми, *I go to him, to her, with him, with her, with them*. But if the genitive case of this pronoun, both singular and plural, is used in the sense of a *possessive* pronoun, then the letter *н* is *not* prefixed. *Ex.* Я былъ у его́ прія́теля, у ей бра́та, и у ихъ сестры́, *I was at his friend's, at her brother's, and their sister's*.

The following are declined in one number only :—

| | | | | | | |
|---|---|---|---|---|---|---|
| N. | И. | *nil* | кто who? | никто́, no one. | что, what. | ничто́, nothing. |
| G. | Р. | себя́, of self. | кого́, | никого́, | чего́, | ничего́. |
| D. | Д. | себѣ́, | кому́, | никому́, | чему́, | ничему́. |
| A. | В. | себя́, | кого́, | никого́, | что, | ничто́. |
| I. | Т. | собо́ю, | кѣмъ, | никѣ́мъ, | чѣмъ, | ничѣ́мъ. |
| P. | П. | о себѣ́, | о комъ, | ни о ко́мъ, | о чёмъ, | ни о чёмъ. |

Кое-кто́, кто-ли́бо, кто-нибу́дь are declined like кто; and кое-что́, что-ли́бо, что-нибу́дь, like что.

(2) Pronouns declined like adjectives :—

| | | *Singular Number.* | | | *Plural Number.* |
|---|---|---|---|---|---|
| Cases. | | Masc. | Fem. | Neut. | All Genders. |
| N. | И. | мой, my, mine. | моя́, | моё. | мои́. |
| G. | Р. | моего́, | мое́й, | моего́. | мои́хъ. |
| D. | Д. | моему́, | мое́й, | моему́. | мои́мъ. |
| A. | В. | {моего́, мой,} | мою́, | моё. | {мои́хъ. мои́.} |
| I. | Т. | мои́мъ, | мое́ю, | мои́мъ. | мои́ми. |
| P. | П. | о моёмъ, | о мое́й, | о моёмъ. | о мои́хъ. |

Твой -я́ -ё -и́, thy, thine, theirs, their; свой -я́ -ё -и́, his, her, its, their own, are declined like мой -я́ -ё -и́.

|  | | Singular Number. | | | Plural Number. |
|---|---|---|---|---|---|
| Cases. | | Masc. | Fem. | Neut. | All Genders. |
| N. | И. | нашъ, our, ours, | наша, | наше. | наши. |
| G. | Р. | нашего, | нашей, | нашего. | нашихъ. |
| D. | Д. | нашему, | нашей, | нашему. | нашимъ. |
| A. | В. | { нашего, нашъ, } | нашу, | наше. | { нашихъ. наши. |
| I. | Т. | нашимъ, | нашею, | нашимъ. | нашими. |
| P. | П. | о нашемъ, | о нашей, | о нашемъ. | о нашихъ. |

Вашъ, -а, -е, -и, is declined like нашъ, -а, -е -и.

|  | | Singular Number. | | | Plural Number. |
|---|---|---|---|---|---|
| Cases. | | Masc. | Fem. | Neut. | All Genders. |
| N. | И. | сей, this, | сія, | сіе. | hese. |
| G. | Р. | сего, | сей, | сего. | сихъ. |
| D. | Д. | сему, | сей, | сему. | симъ. |
| A. | В. | { сего, сей, } | сію, | сіе. | { сихъ. сіи. |
| I. | Т. | симъ, | сею, | симъ. | сими. |
| P. | П. | о сёмъ, | о сей, | о сёмъ. | о сихъ. |

|  | | Singular Number. | | | Plural Number. |
|---|---|---|---|---|---|
| Cases. | | Masc. | Fem. | Neut. | All Genders. |
| N. | И. | тотъ, that, | та, | то. | тѣ, those. |
| G. | Р. | того, | той, | того. | тѣхъ. |
| D. | Д. | тому, | той, | тому. | тѣмъ. |
| A. | В. | { того, тотъ, } | ту, | то. | { тѣхъ. тѣ. |
| I. | Т. | тѣмъ, | тою, | тѣмъ. | тѣми. |
| P. | П. | о томъ, | о той, | о томъ. | о тѣхъ. |

|  | | Singular Number. | | | Plural Number. |
|---|---|---|---|---|---|
| Cases. | | Masc. | Fem. | Neut. | All Genders. |
| N. | И. | этотъ, this, | эта, | это. | эти. |
| G. | Р. | этого, | этой, | этого. | этихъ. |
| D. | Д. | этому, | этой, | этому. | этимъ. |
| A. | В. | { этого, этотъ, } | эту, | это. | { этихъ. эти. |
| I. | Т. | этимъ, | этою, | этимъ. | этими. |
| P. | П. | объ этомъ, | объ этой, | объ этомъ. | объ этихъ. |

| Cases. | Masc. | Fem. | Neut. | Mas. Fem. & Neut. |
|---|---|---|---|---|
| | *Singular Number.* | | | *Plural Number.* |
| N. И. | óный, this or that one, the said, | óная, | óное. | óные, óныя. these or those, the said. |
| G. P. | óнаго, | óной, | óнаго. | óныхъ. |
| D. Д. | óному, | оной, | óному. | óнымъ. |
| A. B. | { óнаго, óный, } | óную, | óное. | { óныхъ. óные, óныя. } |
| I. T. | óнымъ, | óною, | óнымъ. | óными. |
| P. П. | объ óномъ, | объ óной, | объ óномъ. | объ óныхъ. |

| Cases. | Masc. | Fem. | Neut. | All Genders. |
|---|---|---|---|---|
| | *Singular Number.* | | | *Plural Number.* |
| N. И. | чей, whose, | чья, | чьё. | чьи. |
| G. P. | чьего, | чьей, | чьего. | чьихъ. |
| D. Д. | чьему, | чьей, | чьему. | чьимъ. |
| A. B. | { чьего, чей, } | чью, | чьё. | { чьихъ. чьи. } |
| I. T. | чьимъ, | чьею, | чьимъ. | чьими. |
| P. П. | о чьёмъ, | о чьей, | о чьёмъ. | о чьихъ. |

| Cases. | Masc. | Fem. | Neut. | Mas. Fem. & Neut. |
|---|---|---|---|---|
| | *Singular Number.* | | | *Plural Number.* |
| N. И. | какóй, what sort, | какáя. | какóе. | какíе, какíя. |
| G. P. | какóго, | какóй, | какóго. | какихъ. |
| D. Д. | какóму, | какóй, | какóму. | какимъ. |
| A. B. | { какóго, какóй, } | какýю, | какóе. | { какихъ. какíе, какíя. } |
| I. T. | какимъ, | какóю, | какимъ. | какими. |
| P. П. | въ какóмъ, | въ какóй, | въ какóмъ. | въ какихъ. |

Такóй, áя, óе, íе, íя, are declined in the same manner.

| Cases. | Masc. | Fem. | Neut. | All Genders. |
|---|---|---|---|---|
| | *Singular Number.* | | | *Plural Number.* |
| N. И. | самъ, alone, | самá, | самó. | сáми. |
| G. P. | самогó, | самóй, | самогó. | самихъ. |
| D. Д. | самомý, | самóй, | самомý. | самимъ. |
| A. B. | { самогó, самъ, } | { самую, самоё, } | самó. | { самихъ. сáми. } |
| I. T. | самимъ, | самóю, | самимъ. | самими. |
| P. П. | о самóмъ, | о самóй, | о самóмъ. | о самихъ. |

|  | | *Singular Number.* | | | *Plural Number.* |
|---|---|---|---|---|---|
| Cases. | | Masc. | Fem. | Neut. | Mas.Fem.&Neut. |
| N. | И. | сáмый, the very, the self same. | сáмая, | сáмое. | сáмые, сáмыя, these or those very, the self same. |
| G. | Р. | сáмаго, | сáмой, | сáмаго. | сáмыхъ. |
| D. | Д. | сáмому, | сáмой, | сáмому. | сáмымъ. |
| A. | В. | { сáмаго, сáмый, } | сáмую, | сáмое. | { сáмыхъ. сáмые, сáмыя. |
| I. | Т. | сáмымъ, | сáмою, | сáмымъ. | сáмыми. |
| P. | П. | о сáмомъ, | о сáмой, | о сáмомъ. | о сáмыхъ. |

|  | | *Singular Number.* | | | *Plural Number.* |
|---|---|---|---|---|---|
| Cases. | | Masc. | Fem. | Neut. | All Genders. |
| N. | И. | весь, all, the whole. | вся, | всё. | всѣ. |
| G. | Р. | всегó, | всей, | всегó. | всѣхъ. |
| D. | Д. | всему́, | всей, | всему́. | всѣмъ. |
| A. | В. | { всегó, весь, } | всю, | всё. | { всѣхъ. всѣ. |
| I. | Т. | всѣмъ, | всéю, | всѣмъ. | всѣми. |
| P. | П. | обо всёмъ, | па всей, | при всёмъ. | во всѣхъ. |

The pronoun *нѣкто* is used only in the nominative case, and *нѣчто* only in the nominative and accusative cases. *Ex.* Нѣкто ко мнѣ приходи́лъ, *somebody* came to me; Я скажу́ вамъ нѣчто нóвое, I will tell you *something* new. For the other cases of these two pronouns the oblique cases of *кто-тó* and *что-тó* are substituted. *Ex.* Когó-то нѣтъ, *Some one* (is) wanting; комý-то скýчно, *some one* (is) dull; чегó-то не достáетъ, *something* is not obtainable; чѣмъ-то егó наградя́тъ, they will reward him *with something*. All the other pronouns are declined like adjectives with full terminations.

## THE VERB (Глагóлъ).

§ 93. A Verb denotes the action or condition of an object. *Ex.* Хвали́ть, to praise; хвали́ться, to praise one's self, to boast; бытъ хвали́му, to be praised, &c.

§ 94. Verbs are divided, according to their signification, into the following *Voices* (Залóгъ) :—

(1) *Active* (дѣйстви́тельный), which denotes an action that passes from the agent to the object. Now, as the greater part of verbs of the *active* voice require the accusative case, their class can be

ascertained by the questions *Кого?* *Whom?* *Что?* *What?* Ex. Я хвалю (*Кого*)? I praise (*whom*)? *Ans.* Брата, Brother. Я читаю *Что?* I am reading (*what*)? *Ans.* Книгу, a book.

(2) *Neuter* (средній), which, being the opposite of the active voice, denotes some kind of condition or action that does *not* pass from the agent to any object, but which is complete in itself. Ex. Пдти́, to go (*once*); ходи́ть, to go (*more than once*); спать, to sleep; ѣхать, to drive; плакать, to weep.

*Obs.*—(1) The verbs быть, to be, and стать, to become, to begin, which are of the neuter voice, are called *Auxiliary* (вспомогательный) *Verbs*, because they assist in forming the tenses of other verbs. Ex. Я буду читать, I will read; Ты былъ награждёнъ, Thou wast rewarded; Онъ сталъ писать, He began to write. The verb быть when used separately stands in the place of the verbs существовать, to be, to exist, and находиться, to find oneself, to exist, to be. Ex. У него́ есть книги, He has books, *lit.* (there) are books with him; Я былъ у брата, I was at (my) brother's. The verb быть is in such instances called a *Substantive Verb* (существительный глаголъ).

*Obs.*—(2) *All Verbs* which give expression to the call or cry of the several four-footed animals or of birds are of the *neuter* voice. Ex. Левъ рыкаетъ, the lion roars, from рыкать; медвѣдь ревётъ, the bear growls, from ревѣть; собака и лисица лаютъ, the dog and the fox bark, from лаять; ворона каркаетъ, the crow caws, from каркать; сорока щебечетъ, the magpie chatters, from щебетать; лошадь ржетъ, the horse neighs, from ржать; волкъ воетъ, the wolf howls, from выть; быкъ и корова мычатъ, the bull (or ox) and the cow low, from мычать; овца блеетъ, the sheep bleats, from блеять; кошка мяукаетъ, the cat mews, from мяукать; свинья хрюкаетъ, the pig grunts, from хрюкать; голубь воркуетъ, the pigeon coos, from воркова́ть; курица клокчетъ, the hen clucks, from клохта́ть; лягушка квакаетъ, the frog croaks, from квакать; стрекоза и пчела жужжатъ, the dragon-fly and the bee buzz, from жужжа́ть.

(3) *Reflective* (возвратный), which indicates an action that is reflected back from the object to the agent. The reflective verbs of the Russian language are formed by the union of a verb of the active voice with a contracted form of the reflective pronoun

себя (ся). *Ex.* хвали́ться = хвали́ть себя́, to praise one's self; мы́ться = мыть себя́, to wash one's self.

(4) *Reciprocal* (взаи́мный), which denotes a reciprocal action between the agent and the object or objects. Verbs of this voice also terminate in *ся*. They answer, moreover, to the questions—Съ кѣмъ? *With whom? Ex.* ссо́риться, to quarrel; сража́ться, to fight; &c.

> *Obs.*—There are some verbs without the suffix *ся* that have the meaning of verbs of the reciprocal voice. *Ex.* спо́рить, to dispute; \*игра́ть, to play. All such answer to the question, Съ кѣмъ? *With whom?*

(5) *Common* (о́бщій). These likewise terminate in *ся*, and without the particle they are not used. They have the meaning of verbs of either the active or neuter voice. *Ex.* боя́ться, to fear, to be afraid of; кого́? чего́? *of whom? of what?* повинова́ться, to be obedient to; кому́? чему́? *to whom? to what?* надѣя́ться, to rely on; на кого́, на что? *on whom? on what?* труди́ться, to labour; надъ чѣмъ? *at what?* (The above have the meaning of verbs of the active voice.) Улыба́ться, to smile; очути́ться, to appear; and лѣни́ться, to be lazy; have the meaning of verbs of the neuter voice.

(6) *Passive* (страда́тельный), which betokens the *condition* of one object with the *action* of another. *Ex.* быть люби́му, to be loved, &c. Verbs of the passive voice are formed by joining an active verb with various parts of the auxiliary verb быть. They answer to the questions, кѣмъ? чѣмъ? *by whom? by what?* Sometimes verbs of the passive voice terminate in *ся*. *Ex.* почита́ться, to be respected, &c.

§ 95. Certain verbs, according to the meaning which they convey, are of various voices. *Ex. Active Verb*—Онъ игра́етъ на скри́пкѣ но́вую пѣ́сню, He is playing a new song on the violin. *Neuter Verb*—Онъ не у́чится, а игра́етъ, He does not study, but plays. *Reciprocal Verb*—Я би́лся съ нимъ на рапира́хъ, I fenced with him (*lit.* fought with rapiers with him). *Reflective Verb*—Я до́лго труди́лся надъ э́тою зада́чею, I laboured for a long time over this problem; &c. *Verbs of the Neuter Voice* before which certain prepositions are placed become *Verbs of the Active Voice* :—

*Ex.: Neuter Verb*, идти́, to go;  *Active Verb*, перейти́, to go across.
„  „  ходи́ть, to go;  „  „  обходи́ть, to go *round*.
„  „  спать, to sleep;  „  „  проспа́ть, to *over*sleep.

§ 96. The properties of Russian verbs which render them liable to changes of termination are—*mood* (наклоне́ніе), *tense* (вре́мя), *aspect* (видъ), *person* (лицо́), *number* (число́), *gender* (родъ), *participle* (прича́стіе), *gerund* (дѣеприча́стіе).

§ 97. The mood gives expression to various forms of action or of condition, either in the person or agent.

§ 98. Russian verbs have three moods:—

(1) *Infinitive* (Неопредѣлённое), which does not show *by whom* or *when* the action was performed; *i. e.* which does not point out the time, or number and gender of the person or persons, at which, and by whom, the action was performed. *Ex.* писа́ть, to write; сража́ться, to fight; &c.

(2) *Indicative* (Изъяви́тельное), which shows *by whom* and *when* the action was performed—which shows, in fact, the time and number, and even the gender, of the person or persons, at which, and by whom, the action was performed. *Ex.* Я пишу́, I am writing; ты сража́лся, thou foughtest; она́ игра́ла, she played; &c.

(3) *Imperative* (Повели́тельное), which conveys an order, wish, or prohibition, for or against a thing being done. *Ex.* пиши́, write (thou); пусть онъ дѣлаетъ, let him do (it); не сража́йтесь, do not (you) fight; &c.

> *Obs.*—In order to express by means of a Russian verb the *subjunctive* (сослага́тельное), or *conditional* (усло́вное), *mood*, which is in use in foreign languages, the conjunction бы is added to the past tense of the verb in question. *Ex.* Я ко́нчилъ бы э́то дѣ́ло, если бы имѣ́лъ досу́гъ, I *would have* finished this business if I *had had* time; &c.

§ 99. The tense of a Russian verb shows either that the action of the agent is *now* taking place, or that it has taken place at some time or other *before*, or that it *will* yet take place. And therefore a Russian verb has three tenses, viz. *present* (настоя́щее), *past* (прошéдшее), and *future* (бýдущее).

§ 100. The aspect of a Russian verb shows the difference of time required for the performance of an action. *Ex.* онъ рѣша́лъ, he *was deciding;* онъ рѣши́лъ, he *has decided;* онъ кри́кнулъ, he shouted (*once*); онъ хáживалъ, he used to walk (*habitually*).

§ 101. Russian verbs have four Aspects: (1) *imperfect* (несовершéнный); (2) *perfect* (совершéнный); (3) *perfect of unity* (однокрáтный); (4) *iterative* (многокрáтный). The *present* tense has *no* aspects. The *past* tense *may* have all *four*. The *future* tense has *three*, viz. *imperfect, perfect,* and *perfect of unity*.

§ 102. The signification of the several aspects is as follows:—

(1) The imperfect aspect denotes either that the action has not altogether ceased, or that it will not finish. *Ex.* Я писа́лъ, I wrote; Я бýду писа́ть, I will be writing; &c.

(2) The *perfect aspect* denotes either that the action has been *quite* completed, or that it will definitely cease. *Ex.* Я написа́лъ, I have written (*once for all*); Я напишý, I will write (*finally*).

(3) The *aspect of the perfect of unity* denotes either that the action has taken place or will take place *once*, and that *rapidly*. *Ex.* Ты стýкнулъ, thou hast knocked; Я стýкну, I *am going to* knock.

(4) The *iterative aspect* denotes that the action has taken place several times. *Ex.* Я чи́тывалъ, I used (*often*) to read; Онъ хáживалъ, He *was in the habit of* walking.

> *Obs.*—Russian verbs admit, too, of a *fifth* aspect being added, that of the *inchoative* (начина́тельный). This aspect denotes that any sort of action has merely been *begun*. *Ex.* Я запѣ́лъ = Я нáчалъ пѣть, I began to sing; Онъ заигра́етъ = Онъ начнётъ игрáть сію минýту, He will begin to play this minute; Вѣтеръ подýлъ = вѣтеръ нáчалъ дуть, The wind began to blow.

§ 103. The *infinitive mood* does not indicate the time at which an action takes place, yet it has all four aspects: (1) *imperfect*, стучáть, to knock; (2) *perfect*, постучáть, to knock *a little;* (3) *perfect of unity*, стукнýть, to *give a* knock; (4) *iterative*, стýкивать, to knock *repeatedly.*

§ 104. The *indicative mood* comprises all the tenses and all the aspects pertaining to those tenses.

§ 105. The *imperative mood*, although it does not possess tenses, has three aspects: (1) *imperfect*, стучи́, knock (thou); (2) *perfect of unity*, стýкни, knock (thou) *once;* (3) *perfect*, постучи́, knock (thou) *a little.*

§ 106. Russian verbs have three persons, which are usually represented by the personal pronouns:—1st person, я, мы; 2nd person, ты, вы; 3rd person, онъ, онá, онó, онú, онѣ. *Ex.* Я пишý, мы пи́шемъ; *ты* пи́шешь, *вы* пи́шете; онъ писáлъ, онá писáла, онó писáло, онú or онѣ писáли.

§ 107. The two Numbers of Russian Verbs are the Singular and the Plural. The former denotes the *action* or *condition* of one agent or object: *Ex.* Я стрóю, *I* am building (a house). The latter points to the action or condition of two or more agents or objects: *Ex.* Мы стрóимъ, *We* are building (a house).

§ 108. The use of the gender in Russian verbs is confined to the past tense. *Ex.* Я читáлъ, онá читáла, онó и́ли дитя́ читáло, *I* read, *she* read, *it or* the child read.

§ 109. A *participle* is an adjective formed from a verb. *Ex.* Ю́ноша обогащáющій свóй умъ наýками бýдетъ полéзенъ себѣ́ и другимъ, The youth (*who*) *enriches* his intellect with science will be useful to himself and to others. The Russian participle takes the place of two words, viz. the relative pronoun котóрый, who *or* which, and any of the tenses of the indicative mood of a verb; thus, instead of saying Ю́ноша, котóрый обогащáетъ свóй умъ наýками, &c., it is usual to express the sentence in Russian in the way above shown.

§ 110. Participles, being formed from verbs, possess voices, tenses, and aspects; and, as verbal *adjectives*, they possess also genders, numbers, and cases.

§ 111. A *Gerund* is a verb placed in such a form as to contain a meaning which is not complete without the addition of some other verb. *Ex.* Смотря въ окно́, онъ любу́ется прекра́снымъ ви́домъ, *Whilst looking out of the* window, he admires the beautiful view.

§ 112. A Gerund, being part of a verb, has voices, tenses, and aspects.

§ 113. The terminations of Russian verbs are subject to change according to their mood, tense, aspect, person, number, and gender. These changes are called *conjugations* (спряжéнie).

§ 114. Russian verbs have two conjugations. The 2nd person, singular number, present tense, indicative mood, of *regular* Russian verbs of the 1st conjugation *invariably* terminates in *ешь* : *Ex.* Ты чита́ешь, гуля́ешь, проща́ешься. Whereas the corresponding part of a *regular* Russian verb of the 2nd conjugation ends in *ишь* : *Ex.* стои́шь, верти́шь, ко́рмишься.

§ 115. Before considering the conjugation of the other verbs, it may be well to conjugate the auxiliary verb быть, to be.

INFINITIVE MOOD.

Imperfect aspect . . быть, to be.
Iterative aspect . . быва́ть, to be (*often*).

INDICATIVE MOOD.

*Present Tense of* быть.

| *Singular Number.* | | *Plural Number.* | |
|---|---|---|---|
| Я есмь, | I am. | Мы есмы́, | We are. |
| Ты еси́, | Thou art. | Вы есте́, | You are. |
| Онъ ⎫<br>Она́ ⎬ есть,<br>Оно́ ⎭ | ⎧ He ⎫<br>⎨ She ⎬ is.<br>⎩ It ⎭ | Они́ ⎫ суть,<br>Онѣ ⎭ | They are. |

*Obs.*—Есмь, еси́, есмы and есте́, are not in use in modern Russian.

### Present Tense of бывáть.

| | | | | |
|---|---|---|---|---|
| Я бывáю, | I am often. | | Мы бывáемъ, | We are often. |
| Ты бывáешь, | Thou art often. | | Вы бывáете, | You are often. |
| Онъ ⎫<br>Онá ⎬ бывáетъ, | ⎧He ⎫<br>⎨She⎬ is often. | | Онѝ ⎫ бывáютъ, | They are often. |
| Онó ⎭ | ⎩It ⎭ | | Онѣ ⎭ | |

### Past Tense of быть.

| | | | | |
|---|---|---|---|---|
| Я былъ, | I was. | | Мы бы́ли, | We were. |
| Ты былъ, | Thou wast. | | Вы бы́ли, | You were. |
| Онъ былъ, | He was. | | Онѝ ⎫ бы́ли, | They were. |
| Онá былá, | She was. | | Онѣ ⎭ | |
| Онó былó, | It was. | | | |

### Past Tense of бывáть.

| | | | | |
|---|---|---|---|---|
| Я бывáлъ, | I used to be. | | Мы бывáли, | We used to be. |
| Ты бывáлъ, | Thou usedst to be. | | Вы бывáли, | You used to be. |
| Онъ бывáлъ, He ⎫ | | | Онѝ ⎫ бывáли, | They used to be. |
| Онá бывáла, She ⎬ used to be. | | | Онѣ ⎭ | |
| Онó бывáло, It ⎭ | | | | |

### Future Tense of быть.

| | | | | |
|---|---|---|---|---|
| Я бýду, | I will be. | | Мы бýдемъ, | We will be. |
| Ты бýдешь, | Thou wilt be. | | Вы бýдете, | You will be. |
| Онъ ⎫<br>Онá ⎬ бýдетъ, | ⎧He ⎫<br>⎨She⎬ will be. | | Онѝ ⎫ бýдутъ, | They will be. |
| Онó ⎭ | ⎩It ⎭ | | Онѣ ⎭ | |

### THE IMPERATIVE MOOD.

| | |
|---|---|
| Бýдь ты, Be thou. | Бýдьте, Be you. |
| Пусть онъ, онá, онó, бýдетъ,<br>Let him, her, or it, be. | Пусть онѝ, онѣ, бýдутъ,<br>Let them be. |

### PARTICIPLES.

Present of быть . . . сýщій -ая -ее -іе -ія,* who, or which, is, or are.
Present of бывáть . . бывáющій -ая -ее -іе -ія, who, or which, is, or are.
Past of быть . . . . бы́вшій -ая -ее -іе -ія, who, or which, was, or were.
Past of бывáть . . . бывáвшій -ая -ее -іе -ія, who, or which, used to be.
Future of быть . . . бýдущій -ая -ее -іе -ія, who, or which, will be.

### GERUNDS.

Present of быть . . . бýдучи, being.
Past of быть . . . бывъ, бы́вши, having been.
Past of бывáть , . . бывáвъ, бывáвши, having *often* been.

---

\* Ancient Slavonic form, сый -ая -ое -ые -ыя.

§ 116. The auxiliary verb стать, to become, to begin, has only two tenses, viz. the future, я стану, and the past, я сталъ. The first of these is used in place of the same tense of the verb быть (я буду): *Ex.* Я стану, *or* Я буду, писáть, I will write. The second in place of the same tense of the verb начáть, to begin: *Ex.* Я сталъ, *or* Я начáлъ, писáть, I began to write.

§ 117. The regular Russian verbs are conjugated in the following manner:—

### FORMS OF THE CONJUGATIONS.

#### INFINITIVE MOOD.
(Has no Tenses.)

| ASPECTS. | TERMINATIONS. | EXAMPLES. | |
|---|---|---|---|
| Imperfect . . . . | ать, чь, ти. | рѣшáть, | to decide. |
| | | печь, | to bake. |
| | | нести́, | to carry. [all. |
| Perfect . . . . . | ить, чь, ти. | рѣши́ть, | to decide, once for |
| | | испéчь, | to bake through. |
| | | понести́, | to carry away. |
| Perfect of Unity . . | путь. | ду́нуть, | to blow. |
| | | сту́кнуть, | to knock. |
| | | дви́нуть, | to move. |
| Iterative . . . . . | ивать, ывáть. | пáшивать, | to sew on. |
| | | дѣлывать, | to do. |

#### INDICATIVE MOOD.
*Present Tense.*

| | Singular Number. | Plural Number. |
|---|---|---|
| The Present Tense has no Aspects. | Я . . . . . . . . . ю, у. | Мы . . . . . . емъ, имъ. |
| | Ты . . . . . . ешь, ишь. | Вы . . . . . . ете, ите. |
| | Онъ } . . . етъ, итъ. | { Они́ } ютъ, утъ, ятъ, атъ. |
| | Онá } | { Онѣ } |
| | Онó } | |

*Past Tense.*

| | | Plural |
|---|---|---|
| Imperfect and Perfect | { Я, Ты, Онъ . . . лъ. | Мы, Вы — |
| | Онá . . . ла. | Они́ — } ли. |
| | Онó . . . ло. | Онѣ — |
| Perfect of Unity . . | { Я, Ты, Онъ-нулъ. | Мы, Вы — |
| | Онá-нула. | Они́ — } нули. |
| | Онó-нуло. | Онѣ — |
| Iterative . . . . . | { Я, Ты, Онъ-ивалъ, ывалъ. | Мы, Вы — |
| | Онá-ивала, ывала. | Они́ — } ивали, ывали. |
| | Онó-ивало, ывало. | Онѣ — |

## Future Tense.

| Aspects. | Terminations. | Examples. |
|---|---|---|
| Imperfect . . . . | Я бу́ду<br>Ты бу́дешь<br>Онъ<br>Она́ } бу́детъ<br>Оно́ } ть, чь, ти. | Мы бу́демъ<br>Вы бу́дете<br>Они́<br>Онѣ } бу́аутъ } ть, чь, ти. |
| Perfect . . . . . | Has the same terminations as the Present Tense. | |
| Perfect of Unity . . | Я . . . . . . . . . . . . . . . . . . .ну.<br>Ты . . . . . . . . . . . . . . . . .пешь.<br>Онъ, Она́, Оно́, . . .петъ. | Мы . . . . . . . . . . .немъ.<br>Вы . . . . . . . . . . . .пете.<br>Они́<br>Онѣ } . . . . . .путъ. |

### Imperative Mood.

(Has no Tenses.)

| | Singular Number. | Plural Number. |
|---|---|---|
| For the Imperfect, Perfect, and Perfect of Unity . . . . | Ты . . . . . . . . . . . . . . .и, ь, й.<br>Пусть, Онъ,<br>Она́, Оно́ } етъ, итъ. | Вы . . . . . . . . .ите, ьте, йте.<br>Пусть, { Они́ . . . . . .ютъ, утъ.<br>Онѣ . . . . . .ятъ, атъ. |

| | Participles. | Gerunds. |
|---|---|---|
| Aspects.<br>The Present Tense has no Aspects. | *Present Tense.*<br>*Singular Number.*<br>Masc. Fem. Neut.<br>-щій, -ая, -ее.<br>*Plural Number.*<br>Masc. Fem. & Neut.<br>-щіе -щія. | *All Numbers and Genders.*<br>-а, -я, -учи, -ючи. |
| For all Aspects. | *Past Tense.*<br>*Singular Number.*<br>Masc. Fem. Neut.<br>-вшій, -ая, -ее.<br>*Plural Number.*<br>Masc. Fem. & Neut.<br>-вшіе, -вшія. | *All Numbers and Genders.*<br>-въ, -ши. |

Verbs which terminate in *ся* are also conjugated according to the above table, by adding *сь* or *ся*. *Ex.* Я занима́юсь, I occupy *myself*; Ты прогу́лнваешься, Thou art taking a walk; Вы смѣётесь, You are laughing; Они́ удивля́ются, They are astonished.

The conjugation of verbs of the passive voice will be explained separately.

§ 118. With regard to the forms of their conjugation, Russian verbs are classed as—

(1) *Regular* (пра́вильный), or such as retain the primary syllable in all their moods, tenses, aspects, and numbers, and which have, in all their parts, regular terminations, according to the ordinary rules for the conjugation of verbs. *Ex.* пишу́, I write; писа́лъ, I wrote; напишу́, I will write; изъясня́ю, I am explaining; изъясня́лъ, I explained; изъясни́лъ, I explained *once for all*; изъясню́, I will explain; &c.

(2) *Irregular* (непра́вильный), or such as do not everywhere retain their primary syllable, and which in their terminations depart from the ordinary rules for the conjugation of verbs. *Ex.* иду́, шёлъ, пойду́ (from идти́, to go); ѣмъ, ѣлъ, (from ѣсть, to eat); беру́ (from брать, to take); взялъ and возьму́ (from взять, to take); ложу́сь (from ложи́ться, to lie down); лёгъ and ля́гу (from лечь, to lie down); &c.

(3) *Those conveying a sense of fullness* (изоби́льный), or such as have in the present tense two distinct terminations conveying the self-same meaning. *Ex.* дви́жу and двига́ю, I move; стра́жду and страда́ю, I endeavour; а́лчу and алка́ю, I am hungry; блещу́ and блиста́ю, I shine; машу́ and маха́ю, I am beckoning.

(4) *Defective* (недоста́точный), or such as have not any particular tense or aspect. *Ex.* пойма́ть to catch, очну́ться to wake up, мо́лвить to utter, ра́нить to wound, which have no present tense; or the following, which have no past or future tenses of the perfect aspect:—обожа́ть to worship, ожида́ть to await, опаса́ться to dread, подража́ть to imitate, сожалѣ́ть to commiserate, &c.

(5) *Impersonal* (безли́чный), or such as are used only in the 3rd person. *Ex.* мо́жно (it is) possible, должно́ (it) should be, ка́жется it appears, жаль (it is a) pity, нѣтъ (т. е. не есть) there is not, спится one is drowsy, говори́тся it is said, хо́чется one would like, разсвѣта́етъ it dawns, моро́зитъ it freezes, говоря́тъ they say, &c.

(6) *Frequentative* (учаща́тельный), or such as denote a certain

amount of continuance in the time of the action which they illustrate. *Ex.* похáживать to walk *up and down,* поглядывать to look *round*, &c.

§ 119. Russian verbs, according to their construction, are also—

(1) *Simple* (простóй), or such as have not prefixed to them prepositions or other words, and which therefore retain their primitive meanings. *Ex.* дѣйствовать to act, носи́ть to carry, ходи́ть to walk, являться, to appear *generally,* &c.

(2) *Compound* (слóжный), or such as have prefixed to them prepositions or other words (in some instances nouns substantive). *Ex.* благотвори́ть to do *good,* злодѣйствовать to do *evil,* содѣйствовать to co-operate, относи́ть to take *away,* разсказывать to narrate, уходи́ть to go *away,* появляться to make one's appearance, &c.

*Obs.*—The greater portion of the *compound* verbs are formed by prefixing prepositions to the iterative aspect of *simple* verbs. *Ex.* передѣлывать to do *over again,* отъѣзжать to ride *away,* раскрáтивать to paint *all over.* Very many *simple* verbs, in order to form their *perfect* aspect, take as prefixes various prepositions, or else borrow the perfect aspect bodily from compound verbs. *Ex.* писáть to write, написáть; стáвить to erect, постáвить; крáсить to colour, вы́красить; цвѣсть to blossom, расцвѣсть; &c.

### Examples of the Conjugations.

#### § 120. *Of the Regular Verbs.*

(1) Conjugation of Verbs of the Active and Neuter Voices:—

| Aspects. | | Infinitive Mood. | | |
|---|---|---|---|---|
| Imperfect . . . | дѣлать. | стучáть. | жить. | ви́дѣть. |
| Perfect . . . . | сдѣлать. | постучáть. | пожи́ть. | уви́дѣть. |
| Perfect of Unity. | —— | стýкнуть. | —— | —— |
| Iterative . . . | дѣлывать. | (not used). | живáть. | ви́дывать. |
| | to do. | to knock. | to live. | to see. |

## Indicative Mood.

### Present Tense. Imperfect Aspect.

| | | | | |
|---|---|---|---|---|
| Я. | дѣлаю. | стучу́. | живу́. | ви́жу. |
| Ты. | дѣлаешь. | стучи́шь. | живёшь. | ви́дишь. |
| Онъ, она́, оно́. | дѣлаетъ. | стучи́тъ. | живётъ. | ви́дитъ. |
| Мы. | дѣлаемъ. | стучи́мъ. | живёмъ. | ви́димъ. |
| Вы. | дѣлаете. | стучи́те. | живёте. | ви́дите. |
| Они́, онѣ́. | дѣлаютъ. | стуча́тъ. | живу́тъ. | ви́дятъ. |
| | I do, &c. | I knock, &c. | I live, &c. | I see, &c. |

### Past Tense.

| Aspects. | | | | |
|---|---|---|---|---|
| Imperfect . . . | дѣлалъ -а -о -лп. | стуча́лъ -а -о -лп. | жилъ -а́ -о́ -лп. | ви́дѣлъ -а -о -лп. |
| Perfect . . . . | сдѣлалъ -а -о -лп. | постуча́лъ -а -о -лп. | пожи́лъ -а́ -о́ -лп. | уви́далъ -а -о -ли. |
| Perfect of Unity . | ——— | сту́кнулъ -а -о -лп. | ——— | ——— |
| Iterative . . . | дѣлывалъ -а -о -лп. | (not used). | жива́лъ -а -о -ли. | ви́дывалъ -а -о -ли. |
| | I did, &c. | I knocked, &c. | I lived, &c. | I saw, &c. |

### Future Tense. Imperfect Aspect.

| | | | | | |
|---|---|---|---|---|---|
| Sing. Num. | я бу́ду<br>ты бу́дешь<br>онъ<br>она́ } будетъ<br>оно́ | дѣлать | or стуча́ть, | or жить, | or ви́дѣть. |
| Plur. Num. | мы бу́демъ<br>вы бу́дете<br>они́ } бу́дутъ<br>онѣ́ | дѣлать, | or стуча́ть, | or жить, | or ви́дѣть. |
| | | I will do, &c. | I will knock, &c. | I will live, &c. | I will see, &c. |

### Future Tense. Perfect Aspect.

| | | | | |
|---|---|---|---|---|
| Singular Number. | я сдѣлаю. | постучу́. | поживу́. | уви́жу. |
| | ты сдѣлаешь. | постучи́шь. | поживёшь. | уви́дишь. |
| | онъ<br>она́ } сдѣлаетъ.<br>оно́ | постучи́тъ. | поживётъ. | уви́дитъ. |
| Plural Number. | мы сдѣлаемъ. | постучи́мъ. | поживёмъ. | уви́димъ. |
| | вы сдѣлаете. | постучи́те. | поживёте. | уви́дите. |
| | они́ } сдѣлаютъ.<br>онѣ́ | постуча́тъ. | поживу́тъ. | уви́дятъ. |
| | I will do, &c. | I will knock, &c. | I will live, &c. | I will see, &c. |

### Perfect of Unity.

| | | | |
|---|---|---|---|
| nil | сту́кну, -ишь, -итъ,<br>-имъ, -ите, -утъ. | nil | nil |
| | I will knock, &c. | | |

## IMPERATIVE MOOD.
### Imperfect Aspect.

| | | | | |
|---|---|---|---|---|
| Sing. Number. | дѣлай | стучи́. | живи́. | nil |
| | пусть {онъ/она́/оно́} дѣлаетъ, or | стучи́тъ, or | живётъ, or | ви́дитъ, let him see, &c. |
| Plur. Number. | дѣлайте | стучи́те. | живи́те. | nil |
| | пусть {они́/онѣ́} дѣлаютъ, or | стуча́тъ, or | живу́тъ, or | ви́дятъ, |
| | do, &c. | knock, &c. | live, &c. | let them see, &c. |

### Perfect Aspect.

| | | | | |
|---|---|---|---|---|
| Sing. Number. | сдѣлай, | постучи́. | поживи́. | nil |
| | пусть {онъ/она́/оно́} сдѣлаетъ, or | постуча́тъ, or | поживётъ. | nil |
| Plur. Number. | сдѣлайте. | постучи́те. | поживи́те. | nil |
| | пусть {они́/онѣ́} сдѣлаютъ, or | постуча́тъ, or | поживу́тъ. | nil |
| | do, &c. | knock, &c. | live, &c. | |

### Perfect of Unity.

| | | | | |
|---|---|---|---|---|
| Sing. Number. | nil | сту́кни, | nil | nil |
| | | пусть {онъ/она́/оно́} сту́кнетъ. | | |
| Plur. Number. | nil | сту́кните. | nil | nil |
| | | пусть {они́/онѣ́} сту́кнутъ. | | |
| | | knock, &c. | | |

## PARTICIPLES.
### Present Tense.

| | | | | | |
|---|---|---|---|---|---|
| Singular Number. | Masc. | Дѣлающій, | стуча́щій, | живу́щій, | ви́дящій. |
| | Fem. | ——щая, | ——щая, | ——щая, | ——щая. |
| | Neut. | ——щее, | ——щее, | ——щее, | ——щее. |
| Plural Number. | Masc. | ——щіе, | ——щіе, | ——щіе, | ——щіе. |
| | Fem. & Neut. | ——щія, | ——щія, | ——щія, | ——щія. |
| | | He who does, &c. | he who knocks, &c. | he who lives, &c. | he who sees, &c. |

### Past Tense.

| Aspects. | | | | |
|---|---|---|---|---|
| Imperfect . . . | дѣлавшій, | стуча́вшій, | жи́вшій, | ви́дѣвшій. |
| | -ая, -ее, -шіе, -шія | -ая, -ее, -іе, -ія, | -ая, -ее, -іе, -ія, | -ая, -ее, -іе, -ія. |
| Perfect . . . . | сдѣлавшій, | постуча́вшій, | поживши́й, | уви́девшій. |
| | -ая, -ее, -іе, -ія, | -ая, -ее, -іе, -ія, | -ая, -ее, -іе, -ія, | -ая, -ее, -іе, -ія. |
| Perfect of Unity . | nil | сту́кнувшій, | nil | nil. |
| | | -ая, -ее, -іе, -ія. | | |
| Iterative . . . | дѣлывавшій, | (not used), | жива́вшій, | ви́дывавшій, |
| | -ая, -ее, -іе, -ія, | | -ая, -ее, -іе, -ія, | -ая, -ее, -іе, -ія. |
| | he who did, &c. | he who knocked, &c. | he who lived, &c. | he who saw, &c. |

## Gerund.

### Present Tense.

| All Numbers and Genders. | дѣлая, doing. | стуча́, knocking. | живя́, living. | видя, seeing. |
|---|---|---|---|---|

### Past Tense.

| Aspects. | | | | |
|---|---|---|---|---|
| Imperfect . . . | дѣл {а́въ, а́вши,} | стуч {а́въ, а́вши,} | жи́вши, | видѣ {въ, вши.} |
| Perfect . . . . | сѣл {а́въ, а́вши,} | постуч {а́въ, а́вши,} | пожи́вши, | увидѣ {въ, вши.} |
| Perfect of Unity . | nil. | сту́кн {увъ, упши,} | nil. | nil. |
| | having done. | having knocked. | having lived. | having seen. |

## (2) Conjugation of Verbs of the Reflective, Reciprocal and Common Voices:—

### Infinitive Mood.

| Aspects. | | | |
|---|---|---|---|
| Imperfect . . . | хвали́ться, | сража́ться, | улыба́ться. |
| Perfect . . . . | похвали́ться, | срази́ться, | nil. |
| Perfect of Unity . | nil. | nil. | улыбну́ться. |
| | to praise one's self. | to fight. | to smile. |

### Indicative Mood.

#### Present Tense.

| Singular Number. | я хвалю́сь, | сража́юсь, | улыба́юсь. |
|---|---|---|---|
| | ты хва́лишься, | сража́ешься, | улыба́ешься. |
| | онъ, она́, оно́ } хва́лится, | сража́ется, | улыба́ется. |
| Plural Number. | мы хва́лимся, | сража́емся, | улыба́емся. |
| | вы хва́литесь, | сража́етесь, | улыба́етесь. |
| | они́, онѣ } хва́лятся, | сража́ются, | улыба́ются. |
| | I praise myself, &c. | I fight, &c. | I smile, &c. |

#### Past Tense.

| Aspects. | | | |
|---|---|---|---|
| Imperfect. . . . | хвали́лся, -лась, -лось, -лись, | сража́лся, -лась, -лось, -лись, | улыба́лся, -лась, -лось, -лись. |
| Perfect . . . . | похвали́лся, -лась, -лось, -лись, | срази́лся, -лась, -лось, -лись. | nil. |
| Perfect of Unity . | nil. | nil. | улыбну́лся, -лась, -лось, -лись. |
| Iterative . . . | хва́ливался, -валась, -валось, -вались. | nil. | nil. |
| | I praised myself, &c. | I fought, &c. | I smiled, &c. |

F

## Future Tense.
### Imperfect Aspect.

Singular Number.  
я бу́ду  
ты бу́дешь,  
онъ  
она́ } бу́детъ,  
оно́  

Plural Number.  
мы бу́демъ,  
вы бу́дете,  
они́  
онѣ } бу́дутъ,  

хвали́ться, *or* сража́ться, *or* улыба́ться,  
I will praise myself, &c.    I will fight, &c.    I will smile, &c.

### Perfect Aspect.

Singular Number.  
я —— похвалю́сь, *or* сражу́сь.  
ты —— похва́лишся, *or* срази́шься.  
онъ  
она́ —— похва́лится, *or* срази́тся.  
оно́  

Plural Number.  
мы —— похва́лимся, *or* срази́мся.  
вы —— похва́литесь, *or* срази́тесь.  
они́  
онѣ —— похва́лятся, *or* сразя́тся.  

I will praise my- I will fight, &c.  
self, &c.

*nil.*

Perfect of Unity.   *nil.*   *nil.*   *nil.*   я улыбну́сь,  
I will smile, &c.

## IMPERATIVE MOOD.
### Imperfect Aspect.

хвали́сь, ——   сража́йся, ——   улыба́йся.  
пусть { онъ / она́ / оно́ } хвали́тся,   пусть { онъ / она́ / оно́ } сража́ется,   пусть { онъ / она́ / оно́ } улыба́ется.

хвали́тесь,   сража́йтесь,   улыба́йтесь.  
пусть { они́ / онѣ } хва́лятся,   пусть { они́ / онѣ } сража́ются,   пусть { они́ / онѣ } улыба́ются.

Praise thyself, &c.   Fight thou, &c.   Smile thou, &c.

### Perfect Aspect.

похвали́сь, ——   срази́сь.  
пусть { онъ / она́ / оно́ } похва́лится, пусть { онъ / она́ / оно́ } срази́тся.

похвали́тесь, ——   срази́тесь.  
пусть { они́ / онѣ } похва́лятся, пусть { они́ / онѣ } сразя́тся.

*nil.*

Praise thyself, &c.   Fight thou, &c.

( 67 )

#### Perfect of Unity.

| | | | |
|---|---|---|---|
| *nil.* | *nil.* | пусть {онъ, она́, оно́} | улыбни́сь. улыбнётся. |
| *nil.* | *nil.* | пусть {они́, онѣ} | улыбни́тесь. улыбну́тся. |

Smile thou, &c.

### Participle.
#### Present Tense.

| | | | | |
|---|---|---|---|---|
| Sing. Num. | Masc. | хвалящійся, | сражающійся, | улыбающійся. |
| | Fem. | ——аяся, | ——щаяся, | ——щаяся |
| | Neut. | ——еeся, | ——щееся, | ——щееся. |
| Plur. Num. | Masc. | ——іеся, | ——щіеся, | ——щіеся. |
| | Fem. & Neut. | ——іяся, | ——щіяся, | ——щіяся. |
| | | he who praises himself, &c. | he who fights, &c. | he who smiles, &c. |

Aspects.            Past Tense.
Imperfect.

| | | | | |
|---|---|---|---|---|
| Sing. Num. | Masc. | хвали́вшійся, | сража́вшійся, | улыба́вшійся. |
| | Fem. | ——шаяся, | ——шаяся, | ——шаяся. |
| | Neut. | ——шееся, | ——шееся, | ——шееся. |
| Plur. Num. | Masc. | ——шіеся, | ——шіеся, | ——шіеся. |
| | Fem. & Neut. | ——шіяся, | ——шіяся, | ——шіяся. |

Perfect.

| | | | | |
|---|---|---|---|---|
| Sing. Num. | Masc. | похвали́вшійся | срази́вшійся. | |
| | Fem. | ——шаяся, | ——шаяся. | |
| | Neut. | ——шееся, | ——шееся. | *nil.* |
| Plur. Num. | Masc. | ——шіеся, | ——шіеся. | |
| | Fem. & Neut. | ——шіяся, | ——шіяся. | |

Perfect of Unity.

| | | | | |
|---|---|---|---|---|
| Sing. Num. | Masc. | | | улыбну́вшійся. |
| | Fem. | | | ——шаяся. |
| | Neut. | *nil.* | *nil.* | ——шееся. |
| Plur. Num. | Masc. | | | ——шіеся. |
| | Fem. & Neut. | | | ——шіяся. |
| | | he who praised himself, &c. | he who fought, &c. | he who smiled, &c. |

### Gerund.
#### Present Tense.

| | | | |
|---|---|---|---|
| All Numbers and Genders. | хваля́сь, praising himself. | сража́ясь, fighting. | улыба́ясь. smiling |

| Aspects. All Numbers and Genders. | Past Tense. | | |
|---|---|---|---|
| Imperfect . . . | хвали́вшись, | сража́вшись, | улыба́вшись. |
| Perfect . . . . | { похвали́вшись, похвали́сь, } | { срази́вшись, срази́сь. } | nil. |
| Perfect of Unity . | nil. | nil. | улыбну́вшись. |
|  | having praised himself. | having fought. | having smiled. |

### (3) Conjugation of Verbs of the Passive Voice :—

| Aspects. | Infinitive Mood. | | | | |
|---|---|---|---|---|---|
| Imperfect . . . | быть хвали́му, | or | награжда́ему, | or | посыла́ему. |
| Perfect . . . . | быть похва́лену, | or | награжде́ну, | or | по́слану. |
| Iterative . . . | быва́ть хвали́му, | or | награжда́ему, | or | посыла́ему. |
|  | to be praised. |  | to be rewarded. |  | to be sent. |

#### Indicative Mood.

*Present Tense.*

Instead of the following antiquated method of conjugating verbs of the present tense and passive voice—Я есмь *or* Я быва́ю хвали́мъ, *or* награжда́емъ, *or* посыла́емъ, &c., I am praised, *or* rewarded, *or* sent, &c.—it is usual to invert the phraseology so as to convert the passive into an active form.

*Ex.* меня́, тебя́, его́, её, насъ, васъ, ихъ } хва́лятъ *or* награжда́ютъ *or* посыла́ютъ, &c., They praise, *or* reward, *or* send me, &c.

*Past Tense.* (Passive Form.)

Imperfect Aspect.

| я, ты, онъ | былъ | хвали́мъ, | *or* | награжда́емъ, | *or* | посыла́емъ. |
|---|---|---|---|---|---|---|
| она́ | была́ | хвали́ма, | *or* | награжда́ема, | *or* | посыла́ема. |
| оно́ | было́ | хвали́мо, | *or* | награжда́емо, | *or* | посыла́емо. |
| мы, вы, они́, онѣ | были | хвали́мы, | *or* | награжда́емы, | *or* | посыла́емы. |

(Active Form.)

меня́, тебя́, его́, её, насъ, васъ, ихъ } хвали́ли, *or* награжда́ли, *or* посыла́ли.

I was praised, &c. *or* rewarded, &c. *or* sent, &c.

| Aspects | | | | | | | |
|---|---|---|---|---|---|---|---|
| Perfect | | | (Passive Form.) | | | | |

| | я<br>ты<br>онъ | } былъ | похва́ленъ, | *or* | награждёнъ, | *or* | по́сланъ. |
|---|---|---|---|---|---|---|---|
| | она́ | была́ | похва́лена, | *or* | награжде́на, | *or* | по́слана. |
| | оно́ | было́ | похва́лено, | *or* | награждено́, | *or* | по́слано. |
| | мы<br>вы<br>они́<br>оне́ | } бы́ли | похва́лены, | *or* | награждены́, | *or* | по́сланы. |

I was praised, &c. *or* rewarded, &c. *or* sent, &c.

(Active Form.)

| | меня́<br>тебя́<br>его́, её<br>насъ<br>васъ<br>ихъ | } | похвали́ли, | *or* | награди́ли, | *or* | посла́ли. |
|---|---|---|---|---|---|---|---|

| Iterative | | | (Passive Form.) | | | | |
|---|---|---|---|---|---|---|---|
| | я<br>ты<br>онъ | } быва́лъ | хвали́мъ, | *or* | награжда́емъ, | *or* | посыла́емъ. |
| | она́ | быва́ла | хвали́ма, | *or* | награжда́ема, | *or* | посыла́ема. |
| | оно́ | быва́ло | хвали́мо, | *or* | награжда́емо, | *or* | посыла́емо. |
| | мы<br>вы<br>они́<br>оне́ | } быва́ли | хвали́мы, | *or* | награжда́емы, | *or* | посыла́емы. |

(Active Form.)

| | меня́<br>тебя́<br>его́, её<br>насъ<br>васъ<br>ихъ | } быва́-<br>ло | хвали́ли,<br>they praised, | *or*<br>*or* | награжда́ли,<br>rewarded, | *or*<br>*or* | посыла́ли.<br>sent me, &c. |
|---|---|---|---|---|---|---|---|

*Aspects.* *Future Tense.*

Imperfect . . . Instead of using the now obsolete form of Я бу́ду хвали́мъ, I will be praised; *or* награжда́емъ, rewarded; *or* посыла́емъ, sent, &c., it is usual to say меня́ бу́дутъ хвали́ть, they will praise; *or* награжда́ть, reward; *or* посыла́ть, send me, &c.

Perfect . . . Я бу́ду похвалёнъ, *or* награждёнъ, *or* по́сланъ, &c. *or* меня́, &c. похва́лятъ, *or* награди́шъ, *or* пошлю́тъ, &c.

IMPERATIVE MOOD.

Imperfect . . . Пусть меня́ хва́лятъ, let me be praised; *or* награжда́ютъ, rewarded; *or* посыла́ютъ, sent, &c.

Perfect . . . Пусть меня́ похва́лятъ, let them praise; *or* награди́тъ, reward; *or* пошлю́тъ, send me, &c.

( 70 )

### PARTICIPLE.

#### Present Tense.

| Aspects. | | | | |
|---|---|---|---|---|
| Sing. Num. | Masc. | хвали́мый, | награжда́емый, | посыла́емый. |
| | Fem. | ——ая, | ——ая, | ——ая. |
| | Neut. | ——ое, | ——ое, | ——ое. |
| Plur. Num. | Masc. | ——ые, | ——ые, | ——ые, |
| | Fem. & Neut. | ——ыя, | ——ыя, | ——ыя. |
| | | he who is praised, &c. | he who is rewarded, &c. | he who is sent, &c. |

#### Past Tense.

**Imperfect.**

| | | | | |
|---|---|---|---|---|
| Sing. Num. | Masc. | хвáленный. | | |
| | Fem. | ——ая. | | |
| | Neut. | ——ое. | *nil.* | *nil.* |
| Plur. Num. | Masc. | ——ые. | | |
| | Fem. & Neut. | ——ыя. | | |

**Perfect.**

| | | | | |
|---|---|---|---|---|
| Sing. Num. | Masc. | похва́ленный, | награждённый, | по́сланный. |
| | Fem. | ——ая, | ——ая, | ——ая. |
| | Neut. | ——ое, | ——ое, | ——ое. |
| Plur. Num. | Masc. | ——ые, | ——ые, | ——ые. |
| | Fem. & Neut. | ——ыя, | ——ыя, | ——ыя. |
| | | he who was praised, &c. | he who was rewarded, &c. | he who was sent, &c. |

### GERUND.

#### Present Tense.

| | | | |
|---|---|---|---|
| All Numbers and Genders. | бу́дучи хвали́мъ, being praised. | *or* награжда́емъ, rewarded. | *or* посыла́емъ. sent. |

#### Past Tense.

| | | | |
|---|---|---|---|
| All Numbers and Genders. | бывъ похва́ленъ, having been praised. | *or* награждёнъ, rewarded. | *or* по́сланъ. sent. |

### § 121. *Conjugation of the Irregular Verbs.*

The following Table exemplifies the manner of conjugating some of the Russian Irregular Verbs:—

| Nos. | INFINITIVE MOOD. | | INDICATIVE MOOD. | | | | IMPERATIVE MOOD. | |
|---|---|---|---|---|---|---|---|---|
| | Imperfect Aspect. | Perfect Aspect. | Present Tense. | | Imperfect. Past. | Perfect. Past. | Perfect. Future. | Imperfect Aspect. | Perfect Aspect. |
| | | | 1st Pers. Sing. | 2nd Pers. Sing. | | | | | |
| 1 | беречь | сберечь, to take care. | берегу́ | бережи́шь | берёгъ | сберёгъ | сберегу́ | береги́ | сбереги́ |
| 2 | брать | взять, to take. [vehicle. | беру́ | берёшь | бралъ | взялъ | возьму́ | бери́ | возьми́ |
| 3 | везти́ | повезти́, to carry, in a | везу́ | везёшь | вёзъ | повёзъ | повезу́ | вези́ | повези́ |
| 4 | вести́ | повести́, to lead. | веду́ | ведёшь | вёлъ | повёлъ | поведу́ | веди́ | поведи́ |
| 5 | влечь | повлечь, to drag. | влеку́ | влечёшь | влёкъ | повлёкъ | повлеку́ | влеки́ | повлеки́ |
| 6 | грызть | изгрызать, to gnaw. | грызу́ | грызёшь | грызъ | изгрызъ | изгрызу́ | грызи́ | изгрызи́ |
| 7 | давать | дать, to give. | даю́ | даёшь | давалъ | далъ | дамъ | давай | дай |
| 8 | идти́ | пойти́, to go. | иду́ | идёшь | шёлъ | пошёлъ | пойду́ | иди́ | поди́ |
| 9 | класть | положи́ть, to put. | кладу́ | кладёшь | клалъ | положи́лъ | положу́ | клади́ | положи́ |
| 10 | лазить | поль́зть, to climb. | ль́зу | ль́зешь | ль́зъ | полье́зъ | полье́зу | ль́зъ | полье́зь |
| 11 | ложи́ться | лечь, to lie down. | ложи́сь | ложи́шся | ложи́лся | лёгъ | ля́гу | ложи́сь | ля́гъ |
| 12 | мочь | смочь, to be able. | могу́ | мо́жешь | мо́гъ | смо́гъ | смогу́ | nil | nil |
| 13 | пести́ | понести́, to carry. | несу́ | несёшь | нёсъ | понёсъ | понесу́ | неси́ | понеси́ |
| 14 | облека́ть | облечь, to clothe. | облека́ю | облека́ешь | облека́лъ | обле́къ | облеку́ | облека́й | облеки́ |
| 15 | обрека́ть | обречь, to condemn. | обрека́ю | обрека́ешь | обрека́лъ | обре́къ | обреку́ | обрека́й | обреки́ |
| 16 | пасти́ | nil | пасу́ | пасёшь | пасъ | nil | nil | паси́ | nil |
| 17 | печь | испечь, to bake. | пеку́ | печёшь | пёкъ | испёкъ | испеку́ | пеки́ | испеки́ |
| 18 | расти́ | вы́рости, to grow. | расту́ | растёшь | ро́съ | вы́росъ | вы́росту | расти́ | вы́рости |
| 19 | сади́ться | сесть, to sit down. | сажу́сь | сади́шся | сади́лся | сълъ | ся́ду | сади́сь | сядь |
| 20 | стеречь | постеречь, to watch. | стерегу́ | стережёшь | стерёгъ | постерёгъ | постерегу́ | стереги́ | постереги́ |
| 21 | спаса́ть | спасти́, to save. | спаса́ю | спаса́ешь | спаса́лъ | спасъ | спасу́ | спаса́й | спаси́ |
| 22 | стричь | остри́чь, to shew. | стригу́ | стрижёшь | стри́гъ | остри́гъ | остригу́ | стриги́ | остриги́ |
| 23 | счечь | вы́счечь, to hew. | счу́ | счёшь | съкъ | вы́счекъ | вы́счку | съки́ | вы́счки |
| 24 | отверга́ть | отвергнуть, to cast away. | отверга́ю | отверга́ешь | отверга́лъ | отвергъ | отвергну | отверга́й | отверга́й |
| 25 | отверза́ть | отверзать, to open. | отверза́ю | отверза́ешь | отверза́лъ | отвёрзъ | отверзу́ | отверза́й | отверза́й |
| 26 | тереть | потере́ть, to rub. | тру | трёшь | тёръ | потёръ | потру́ | три | потри́ |
| 27 | трясти́ | потрясти́, to shake. | трясу́ | трясёшь | трясъ | потря́съ | потрясу́ | тряси́ | потряси́ |
| 28 | умирать | умере́ть, to die. | умира́ю | умира́ешь | умира́лъ | у́меръ | умру́ | умира́й | умри́ |
| 29 | ѣсть | съѣсть, to eat up. | ѣмъ, ѣшь, ѣстъ, ѣдимъ, ѣдите, ѣдятъ. | ѣшь | ѣлъ | съѣлъ | съѣмъ | ѣшь | съѣшь |
| 30 | ѣхать | поѣхать, to ride, or drive. | ѣду, ѣдешь, ѣдетъ, ѣдемъ, ѣдете, ѣдутъ. | | ѣхалъ | поѣхалъ | поѣду | nil | поѣжжа́й |

N.B.—Those verbs which are printed in italics entirely deviate from the general rule.

*Obs.*—Of the irregular verbs inserted in this Table, only two are used in the Aspect of the Perfect of Unity, viz. (No. 27) трясти́—тряхну́ть, and (No. 22) стричь—стригну́ть; whereas in the Iterative Aspect the following are found:—(No. 3) везти́, (No. 4) вести́—ва́живать, (No. 13) пести́—на́шиватъ, (No. 23) счечь—сѣка́ть, (No. 29) ѣсть—ѣда́ть, (No. 30) ѣхать—ѣзжать. The verb мочь (No. 12) is not used in the future tense of the Imperfect Aspect. One cannot, therefore, say я бу́ду or Мы бу́демъ мочь.

## § 122. Rules for the Conjugation of Russian Verbs.

For the conjugation of Russian Verbs there are many rules, but there are also a large number of exceptions to them. We will note only those rules which may be pronounced steadfast, *i.e.* such as admit of the least number of exceptions.

### I. *Rules for the Infinitive Mood.*

(1) The infinitive mood of Russian Verbs of the imperfect aspect generally ends in *ть* preceded by any of the vowels *а, е, и, о, у, ы, ѣ, я*. *Ex.* читáть, to read; терéть, to rub; хвалить, to praise; колóть, to prick; тонýть, to sink; рыть, to dig; имѣть, to have; забавлять, to amuse. We also find the same termination *ть* preceded by the consonants *з* and *с*. *Ex.* лѣзть, to climb; грызть, to gnaw; плесть, to plait; цвѣсть, to bloom. A very few verbs have their infinitive mood in *чь* and *ти*; such as влечь, to drag; идти́, to go (on foot).

(2) The infinitive mood of Russian Verbs of the perfect aspect likewise generally ends in *ть*. This termination has, however, various prefixes. Some verbs form their perfect aspect in a way peculiar to themselves—

| | | |
|---|---|---|
| *Ex.* отличáть, | отличи́ть, | to distinguish. |
| принимáть, | приня́ть, | to receive. |
| одѣвáть, | одѣть, | to dress. |
| брать, | взять, | to take. |

Others, in order to form their perfect aspect, take as prefixes various prepositions:

| | | |
|---|---|---|
| *Ex.* любить, | полюби́ть, | to love. |
| писáть, | написáть, | to write. |

Others, again, borrow a perfect aspect from compound verbs analogous to themselves:

| | | |
|---|---|---|
| *Ex.* берéчь, | сберéчь, | to guard (which is from the verb сберегáть). |
| готóвить, | приготóвить, | to prepare (which is from the verb приготовля́ть). |
| смотрѣть, | посмотрѣть, | to behold (which is from the verb посмáтривать). |

(3) The infinitive mood of verbs of the aspect of the perfect of unity ends in *путь*. *Ex.* мигнýть, to wink; свиснуть, to give a whistle; дёрнуть, to give a pull.

(4) The infinitive mood of verbs of the iterative aspect ends in *ивать* and *ывать*. *Ex.* хáживать, to *be in the habit of* walking; вѝдывать, to *be in the habit of* seeing; читывать, to read *often*.

> *Note.*—But few Russian verbs have the iterative aspect, which can in good style and conversation be used, and therefore this aspect should be employed with great discernment. Verbs ending in *ивать* and *ывать* cannot have an iterative aspect. *Ex.* разсмáтривать, to examine; обязывать, to oblige, &c.

## II. *Rules for the Indicative Mood.*

(1) The first person singular number, present tense, has two terminations, viz. in *ю* and *у*. Before the latter there is always a consonant. *Ex.* идý, I go; сижý, I sit down. The terminations of the second person of the same number and tense are in *ешь* and *ишь* respectively, and those of the third person of the same number and tense in *етъ* and *итъ*. The terminations of the first person, plural number, present tense, are *емъ* and *имъ*; of the second person of the same number and tense *ете, ите*; of the third person of the same number and tense (of verbs of the first conjugation only) *ютъ* or *утъ*. Thus it will be found that the second person of the singular number, present tense, of verbs of the first conjugation has *ешь* for its termination; and so the third person of the plural number, present tense, of verbs of this conjugation will end in *ютъ* or *утъ*. *Ex.* читáешь, thou readest; читáютъ, they read; ведёшь, thou leadest; ведýтъ, they lead; similarly the second person of the same number and tense of verbs of the second conjugation has *ишь*. Consequently the third person of the plural number will be in *атъ* or *ятъ*: *Ex.* молчишь, thou art silent; молчáтъ, they are silent; смóтришь, thou gazest; смóтрятъ, they gaze. Amongst verbs of the second conjugation there are two only which do not follow this rule, viz., бѣжишь, thou runnest; бѣгýтъ, they run (not бѣжáтъ); хóчешь, thou desirest; хотятъ, they desire (not хóчутъ).

(2) Verbs which terminate in the first person, singular number, of the present tense in *ту*, change *т* in the second and third persons

singular, and in the first and second persons plural into *ж*. *Ex*. берегу́, I take care, &c.; бережёшь, бережётъ, бережёмъ, бережёте. In the third person of the plural number they retain the letter *г*; thus, берегу́тъ, стерегу́тъ, they watch.

(3) Verbs which terminate in the first person, singular number, of the present tense in *ку*, change *к* in the second and third persons singular, and in the first and second persons plural, into *ч*. *Ex*. влеку́, I attract; влечёшь, влечётъ, влечёмъ, влечёте.. In the third person of the plural number they retain the letter *к*; thus, влеку́тъ, пеку́тъ, they cook.

(4) Monosyllabic Verbs, which terminate in *итъ*, change *итъ* in the first person singular of the present tense into *ью*. *Ex*. пить, to drink; шить, to sew; вить, to twine; бить, to beat; пью, шью, вью, бью. To this rule the verb брить, to shave, is an exception, as it makes бри́ю, &c.

(5) The present tense is used sometimes in the sense of the future. *Ex*. за́втра Я иду́ въ дере́вню, To-morrow I am going to the village.

(6) The past tense of verbs of the imperfect and perfect aspects terminates in *лъ*. It is formed, as a general rule, from the infinitive mood of the imperfect and perfect aspects by changing *ть* into *лъ*. *Ex*. чита́ть to read, чита́лъ, хотѣть to desire, хотѣлъ; мять to knead, мя́лъ. When the infinitive mood terminates in *чь*, the termination of the past tense is generally found to be either in *къ* or *гъ*. *Ex*. влечъ to attract, влёкъ, бере́чь to guard, берёгъ. Similarly, when the infinitive mood terminates in *сти, зти*, the termination of the past tense is in *съ* or *зъ*. *Ex*. несті́ to bring, нёсъ; взяті́ to carry, вёзъ. The exceptions are: цвѣсті́ to blossom, and вести́ to lead, whose past tenses are цвѣлъ and вёлъ respectively.

(7) The termination of the past tense of verbs of the aspect of perfect of unity is in *нулъ*; thus, мигну́ть to work, makes мигну́лъ.

(8) The termination of the past tense of verbs of the iterative aspect is in *ивалъ* or *ывалъ*. The past tenses of both the perfect of unity and iterative aspects are derived from their respective infinitive moods by changing *ть* into *лъ*: *Ex*. ха́живать, to make a practice of going, ха́живалъ. Verbs which do not possess an iterative aspect replace the want of one by adding the word быва́ло

to the past tense of the imperfect aspect: *Ex.* Я бывáло встрѣчáлъ, I *used to* meet.

(9) The future tense of verbs of the imperfect aspect is formed by prefixing the future tense of the auxiliary verb быть to the infinitive mood of the verb which is being conjugated: *Ex.* Я бýду хвалить, ты бýдешь хвалить, &c., I will praise, &c.

(10) The future tense of verbs of the perfect aspect has the same terminations as has the present tense of verbs of the imperfect aspect. *Ex.* Я похвалю́, ты похвáлишь, &c., I will praise, &c.

(11) The future tense of the aspect of the perfect of unity terminates in *ну, нёшь*, &c. It is formed from the infinitive mood of the same aspect by casting away the final letters *ть*; thus, двинуть, to move, makes двину, двинешь, &c.

### III. *The Imperative Mood.*

(1) As a general rule, only two persons of the imperative mood are used, viz. the 2nd and 3rd: *Ex.* читáй read (ты, *thou*, being understood), пусть онъ, она́ or оно́, чптáетъ, читáйте (вы), пусть они́ or онѣ читáютъ. There are cases, however, in which the 1st person may be used; for example, Будь Я богáтъ, Я бы помо́гъ емý, were I rich, I would assist him. In the same way, the 1st person plural of the present or future tenses of verbs of the perfect aspect is used for the 1st person plural of the imperative mood; thus, идёмъ, ѣдемъ, пойдёмъ, поѣдемъ, let us go, let us eat, &c. In such instances the suffix *те* is frequently added to the 1st person plural of the imperative mood: *Ex.* побѣжи́мте, ся́демте, let us run, let us sit down.

(2) Sometimes the infinitive mood is used in place of the imperative; thus, Молчáть! Не шумѣть! Be silent! Do not make a noise!

(3) In the practice of a high style of conversation or writing, to the 3rd person of the imperative mood is added the particle *да*; for example, *да* вступитъ instead of пусть онъ вступитъ, let him enter.

### IV. *The Participles.*

§ 123. The active participles of verbs of the active and neuter voices terminate as follows:—The present participle in *щій, щая, щее*, for the masc., fem., and neut. genders, respectively. This participle is derived from the 3rd person, plural number, present tense, indicative mood, by changing the final letters *мъ* into *щій* : *Ex.* смо́трятъ, they regard ; смотря́щій, &c., he who regards, &c. The past participle in *вшій, вшая, вшее,* for the masc., fem., and neut. genders, respectively. This participle is derived from the singular number, past tense, indicative mood, by changing *лъ* into *вшій* : *Ex.* смотрѣ́лъ, I regarded ; смотрѣ́вшій, &c., he who regarded, &c. In the case of verbs which have not the letter *л* in the formation of their past tense, the final letter *ъ* of that tense is changed into *шій,* &c. *Ex.* росъ, he grew ; росшій, &c., he who grew, &c. The past participles of the following verbs are as follows :—вести́ to lead, вё.лъ, ве́дшій ; идти́, to go, шёлъ, ше́дшій ; цвѣсти́, to blossom, цвѣ.лъ, цвѣ́тшій ; пасть, to fall, па́лъ, па́дшій.

§ 124. To the terminations of the participles of verbs of the reflective, reciprocal, and common voices, the particle *ся* is added. *Ex.* смотря́щійся, he who regards ; смотрѣ́вшійся, he who regarded ; &c.

§ 125. The participles of verbs of the passive voice are derived only from verbs of the active voice. The present participle of verbs of the passive voice ends in *мый.* This participle is formed from the 1st person, plural number, present tense, indicative mood, of the active voice, by changing the final letter *ъ* into *ый, ая, ее,* (for the masc., fem., and neut. genders respectively). *Ex.* хва́лимъ, we praise ; хвали́мый, &c., he who is praised ; &c. The present passive participles of the following verbs form an exception to this rule :—иска́ть, to seek, иско́мый ; пасти́, to pasture, пасо́мый ; вести́, to lead, ведо́мый. The past participle of verbs of the passive voice ends in *нный* or *тый,* &c. This participle is formed from the singular number, past tense, indicative mood, active voice, by changing the final letters *лъ* of that tense into *нный* or *тый.* *Ex.* дѣ́лалъ, he made, дѣ́ланный, he who is made ; ши.лъ, he sewed ; ши́тое, that which is sewn ; &c. The following verbs form exceptions to the above rule :—хвали́ть, to praise, хва́ленный ; носи́ть, to carry, но́шенный ; проща́ть, to pardon, про́щенный ; забыва́ть, to forget, забы́тый and забве́нный.

> *Obs.*—The present participle of a verb of the passive voice can only be formed by means of either of the two neuter verbs быва́ть and обита́ть.

§ 126. In the Russian language there are no other future participles than that of the verb бытъ, viz. бу́дущій -ая -ее -іе -ія.

§ 127. Participles are declined as nouns adjective.

§ 128. Participles of the passive voice have both full and shortened terminations; thus, from the full forms come the following shortened forms : уважа́емый, -ая -ое, respected, уважа́емъ -а -о ; чи́танный -ая -ое, read, чи́танъ -а -о.

§ 129. As a general rule, participles with full terminations are confined to writing and to books, whereas in conversation the shortened forms of such participles are more often met with. *Ex.* Этотъ домъ хорошо́ постро́енъ, This house (is) well built ; Э́та кни́га прочи́тана, This book (is) read *through ;* Приказа́ніе испо́лнено, The order (is) executed.  In conversation are likewise used such participles as have the meaning of nouns adjective; for instance, Онъ су́щій ребёнокъ, He is a *regular* child ; ра́неный офицеръ, a wounded officer ; непроходи́мый лѣсъ, an impenetrable forest; &c.

## V. *Gerunds.*

§ 130. Gerunds of the present tense of verbs of the active and neuter voices end in *а, я*, or *учи* and *ючи*. *Ex.* стуча́ knocking, си́дя sitting, чита́л or чита́ючи reading, пи́шучи writing.

§ 131. The gerunds of the past tense of such verbs end in *въ* or *вши*. *Ex.* сидѣвъ, сидѣвши, having sat, &c.

§ 132. The first noted terminations of gerunds of either of the above tenses (those in *а, я, въ*) are shortened, whereas those last noted (in *учи, ючи, вши*) are full.  The former are used in ordinary writing and in conversation, the latter in less refined language, or in the vulgar tongue.

§ 133. The gerunds of the present tense, like the participles of the same tense, are formed from the 3rd person, plural number, present tense, indicative mood, of the verb, by changing *атъ* into *а*, and *ятъ, утъ* and *ютъ* into *я*. *Ex.* молча́тъ they are silent, мо́лча ; хо́дятъ, they go, хо́дя ; веду́тъ, they lead, ведя́ ; жела́ютъ, they wish, жела́я.

§ 134. The gerunds of the past tense are formed from past

participles by changing the termination *вший* into *ши* or *въ*. *Ex.* молча́вший, молча́вши, молча́въ, having been silent ; написа́вший, or написа́вши, having written.

§ 135. In the case of verbs of the reflective, reciprocal, and common voices, the particles *сь* and *ся* are respectively added to the shortened form of gerunds of the present tense, and to the full forms of gerunds of the past tense. *Ex.* пря́чась, hiding, спря́тавшись, having hidden, &c.

§ 136. To gerunds of the present tense, passive force (which are but seldom used) is prefixed the future gerund of the auxiliary verb *быть*: *Ex. бу́дучи* хвали́мъ, being praised. In like manner, to gerunds of the past tense, passive voice, the gerund of the past tense of the same verb is prefixed : *Ex. бывъ* хва́ленъ or похва́ленъ, having been praised.

§ 137. Gerunds have sometimes the meanings of adverbs. *Ex.* онъ пи́шетъ *сто́я*, he writes *standing*, &c. Gerunds of this kind are called *verbal adverbs* (отглаго́льное наре́чіе).

## THE ADVERB.

§ 138. An Adverb is generally used with a Verb, in order to show the quality, circumstances, and mode of action. *Ex.* Я шёлъ *ти́хо*, I went *quietly*; Онъ прогу́ливался *вчера́ верхо́мъ*, He went out *yesterday on horseback*. Certain adverbs are also placed before other parts of speech :—(*a*) Examples of those preceding nouns substantive : *мно́го* трудо́въ, *many* labours ; *не́сколько* солда́тъ, *several* soldiers ; *взамѣнъ* де́негъ, *in lieu* of money ; *вмѣсто* книгъ, *in place of* books.—(*b*) Examples of those preceding nouns adjective: онъ *о́чень* приле́жепъ, he is *very* industrious ; *весьма́* поле́зная книга, an *exceedingly* useful book.—(*c*) Examples of adverbs coupled with others, in order to intensify the meaning which it is desired should be conveyed : *весьма́* хорошо́, *exceedingly* good ; *о́чень* бли́зко, *very* near ; *гора́здо* ра́нѣе, *much* earlier ; *едва́* примѣ́тно, *scarcely* perceptible.

§ 139. According to their respective significations, adverbs are classed as follows :—

(1) *Adverbs of Quality :*—These denote the quality or mode of action, in answer to the questions какъ ? how ? каки́мъ о́бразомъ ?

in what manner? *Ex.* Я провожу́ (from провожда́ть) вре́мя хорошо́, I pass time *well;* Ты всё дѣлаешь какъ нибу́дь, Thou doest everything *anyhow;* Онъ лю́битъ прогу́ливаться пѣшко́мъ, He likes to take his exercise *on foot;* &c.

(2) *Adverbs of Quantity:*—(*a*) Answering to the question, ско́лько? how much? how many? *Ex.* мно́го, ма́ло, нѣ́сколько, одна́жды, &c.—(*b*) Answering to the question, во-ско́лько? how many times? *Ans.* вдво́е two-fold, впя́теро five-fold, &c.—(*c*) Answering to the question, на-ско́лько? into how many times? *Ans.* на-дво́е in two, на-че́тверо, into four, &c.

(3) *Adverbs of Place:*—These answer to the questions—*гдѣ?* where? куда́? whither? отку́да? whence? from what place? *Answers:* здѣсь here, тутъ here *or* there, та́мъ there, вездѣ́ everywhere, нигдѣ́ nowhere, гдѣ́-нибу́дь somewhere or other, до́ма at home, туда́ thither, сюда́ hither, домо́й homewards, отту́да thence, отсю́да hence, и́здали from afar, снару́жи from without. To this class of adverbs belong also certain nouns substantive, used in the instrumental case, that is, when such signify the way by which one travels: Онъ ѣ́халъ мо́ремъ и доро́гою захвора́лъ, He went *by sea,* and fell ill *on the road.*

(4) *Adverbs of Time:*—These answer to the question, когда́ when? *Answers:* сего́дня to-day, за́втра to-morrow, ны́нѣ at present, днёмъ by day, но́чью by night, пре́жде before, по́слѣ after, ча́сто often, рѣ́дко seldom, ра́но early, по́здно late, &c. To this class of adverbs belong also уже́ already, еще́ still, again, всё always, &c.

(5) *Adverbs of Precedence,* such as сперва́ first, at first, снача́ла first, at first sight, сно́ва anew, опя́ть again, во-пе́рвыхъ, firstly, во-вторы́хъ secondly, &c.

(6) *Adverbs of Intensity and Augmentation,* such as весьма́ extremely, о́чень, гора́здо much, сли́шкомъ too much, кра́йне to the utmost, &c.

(7) *Adverbs denoting diminution or decrease,* such as едва́ scarcely, чуть hardly, наси́лу with difficulty, почти́ almost, &c.

(8) *Adverbs denoting sufficiency:* дово́льно enough, по́лно fully, бу́детъ that will do, enough, &c.

(9) *Interrogative Adverbs,* such as когда́? when? зачѣ́мъ?

why? для чего? for what? гдѣ? where? куда? whither? неужели? is it possible? indeed! &c.

(10) *Affirmative Adverbs*, such as подлинно really, indeed, истинно verily, въ самомъ дѣлѣ in fact, да yes, такъ so, дѣйствительно actually, конечно of course, &c.

(11) *Negative Adverbs*, such as не no, нѣтъ not, не такъ not so, никакъ by no means, нимало not at all, нисколько not any, отнюдь by no means, совсѣмъ не and вовсе не not at all, &c.

(12) *Hypothetical Adverbs*, such as по-крайней мѣрѣ at least, авось it is to be hoped, чуть-ли scarcely, врядъ-ли it is doubtful whether, можетъ-быть perhaps, &c.

(13) *Exclusive Adverbs*, such as токмо, только and лишь only, единственно solely, кромѣ besides, &c.

(14) *Adverbs of Comparison*, such as подобно like, наравнѣ on a level, такимъ образомъ in this manner, &c.

(15) *Adverbs denoting disparity or dissimilitude*, such as иначе otherwise, напротивъ on the contrary, на-оборотъ *vice-versá*, &c.

(16) *Adverbs denoting partnership*, such as вмѣстѣ together, вообще in general, generally, за-одно jointly, &c.

(17) *Adverbs denoting exchange*, such as вмѣсто instead of, взамѣнъ, in lieu of, &c.

(18) *Adverbs of illustration*, such as именно namely, то есть that is, какъ-то as follows, напримѣръ for example, &c.

(19) *Adverbs denoting suddenness of action*, such as невзначай unawares, внезапно unexpectedly, вдругъ all at once, мгновенно instantaneously, нечаянно unexpectedly, &c.

(20) *Enclitical Adverbs employed in popular speech*, such as молъ then, де said he, дескать so to say, бишь then, &c.

§ 140. All Adverbs, except the qualifying (качественное), and adverbs of quantity (количественное), are called *circumstantial* (обстоятельственное) adverbs.

§ 141. Adverbs denoting quality, which are derived from qualifying nouns adjective, have degrees of comparison, as, for example, хорошо good, лучше better; весело joyous, веселѣе more joyous, всѣхъ веселѣе merrier than all. Certain of the adverbs, too, which denote quantity, place, and time, have likewise degrees of comparison, such as мно́го much, бо́лѣе more, бо́лѣе всѣхъ more than all, бли́зко near, бли́же nearer, всѣхъ бли́же nearer than all, ра́но early, ра́нѣе earlier, всѣхъ ра́нѣе earlier than all.

## THE PREPOSITION.

§ 142 Prepositions indicate the relationship between objects. *Ex.* учени́къ сѣлъ за столъ, the pupil sat down *at* the table. Prepositions likewise serve to alter the meaning of the words to which they are prefixed: *Ex.* до-хо́дъ income, revenue, у-хо́дъ departure, при-хо́дъ arrival, вос-хо́дъ ascent, перемѣни́ть to alter, размѣни́ть to exchange.

§ 143. Prepositions are classed as separable and inseparable.

§ 144. The separable prepositions require after them the oblique cases noted below :—

   (1) *Genitive:* безъ, безо without, для for, ра́ди for the sake of, до up to, изъ out of, отъ away from, у at, изъ-за from behind, изъ-подъ from under.
   (2) *Dative:* къ, ко to, towards.
   (3) *Accusative:* про concerning, чрезъ, че́резъ through, across. сквозь through.
   (4) *Instrumental:* надъ, надо over.
   (5) *Prepositional:* при near, in the presence of.
   (6) *Genitive* or *Instrumental:* ме́жду, межъ between, among.
   (7) *Accusative* or *Instrumental:* за behind *or* for, подъ under, at, предъ, передъ before.
   (8) *Accusative* or *Prepositional:* въ, во in, into, на on, upon, against, о, объ, обо about.
   (9) *Genitive, Accusative* or *Instrumental:* съ, со from, with, together with.
   (10) *Dative, Accusative* or *Prepositional:* по by, up to, after.

§ 145. Amongst the class of separable prepositions may be reckoned also certain adverbs of place which govern the genitive case. *Ex.* близъ near to, во́злѣ beside, по́длѣ along, near, о́коло about, про́тивъ opposite to, ми́мо by, среди́ in the midst of, впереди́ in front of, позади́ behind.

§ 146. The inseparable prepositions are воз, вы, низ, пере, пре and раз. They do not alter the cases of the nouns which follow them, but they change the meaning of the word to which they are prefixed : *Ex*. гóдный suitable, выгодный profitable, мѣна exchange, перемѣна alteration, стрóить to build, разстрóить to *dis*arrange.

## THE CONJUNCTION.

§ 147. A conjunction serves to connect either words or whole sentences. *Ex*. Ивáнъ *и* Пётръ пришлú, John *and* Peter came; Если я бýду здорóвъ *то* приѣду къ вамъ, If I *am* well, *then* I will come to you; Онъ *или* не хóчетъ *или* не мóжетъ помóчь мнѣ, He *either* does not wish to, *or* cannot, help me.

§ 148. Conjunctions are divided into the following :—

(1) *Copulative* (соедини́тельный), such as и and, даже even, притóмъ with this, не тóкмо and не тóлько not only, сверхъ-тогó besides which, тáкже likewise, же but, &c.

(2) *Partitive* (раздѣли́тельный) : и́ли and ли́бо or, &c.

(3) *Explanatory* (изъясни́тельный) : что that, бýдто as if, вѣдь then, now you must know, тогдá какъ whilst, такъ что so that, такъ какъ as, &c.

(4) *Reiterative* (повтори́тельный) : ни-ни neither—nor, чáстію and отчáсти partly, то-то now—then, &c.

(5) *Comparative* (сравни́тельный) : какъ—такъ as—so, скóль-стóль as much—so much, нéжели than, чѣмъ—тѣмъ the more— the less, тáкъ-же—какъ both—and, &c.

(6) *Conditional* (услóвный) or *Suppositional* (предположи́тельный) : éжели, éсли if, чтóбы in order to, дáбы in order that, когдá бы whenever, то бы in order that, то then, therefore, &c.

(7) *Concessional* (уступи́тельный) : хотя́ although, пусть be it so, пускáй so be it, пожáлуй if you like, &c.

(8) *Causal* (винослóвный) : и́бо for, для тогó что for the reason that, because, потомý что because, &c.

(9) *Antithetical* (противополóжный) : но but, однáко however, впрóчемъ furthermore, *a* but, &c.

(10) *Conclusive* (заключи́тельный): ита́къ thus, посему́ for this reason, сле́довательно and ста́ло быть consequently, наконе́цъ finally, at last, &c.

To the class of disjunctive conjunctions belongs likewise the particle ли, which is affixed to a word in order to express a question. *Ex.* Бы́ли ли вы въ Москве́? *Have you* been in Moscow? Томъ ли это домъ? *Is that* the house?

## THE INTERJECTION.

§ 149. Interjections are exclamations[1] which serve to express various feelings.

§ 150. Their classification is as follows:—

(1) of surprise: и! ахъ! ахти́! ба! ба! ой-ли! is it possible!
(2) of approval: ай-да! испола́ть! hail! то-то? бра́во!
(3) of joy: ура́!
(4) of assurance: ей-ей! пра́во! right!
(5) of call: эй! гей!
(6) the answer to a call: а! ась! что! ау!
(7) of laughter: ха! ха! хи! хи!
(8) of indignation: тьфу! фуй!
(9) of incitement: ну! ну-те!
(10) those which imply a proposal: на! на-те!
(11) of fear: ой! ахти!
(12) of threat: ужъ! вотъ! добро!
(13) of reproach: э! эхъ! ну-ужъ!
(14) of prohibition: тсъ! цыцъ!
(15) of sorrow and commiseration: охъ! увы!
(16) of indication: вотъ! вонъ!

§ 151. Interjections likewise serve to express various sounds. *Ex.* бухъ! павъ! хлопъ! динь-динь-динь!

---

[1] As such exclamations are, for the most part, mere sounds, they cannot well be represented in every instance in another language. *Trans.*

# SECOND PART

(Отдѣле́ніе Второ́е).

## SYNTAX.

§ 152. Syntax expounds the rules for employing words so as to form intelligible speech.

§ 153. Speech is the expression of our thoughts by means of words.

§ 154. A short sentence expressed in words is called a *proposition* (предложе́ніе). *Ex.* Безкоры́стіе есть доброде́тель, disinterestedness is (a) virtue; го́рдость поро́къ, pride (is a) vice; они́ бу́дутъ бога́ты, they will be rich; &c.

§ 155. The proposition consists of two principal parts—the *subject* (подлежа́щее) and the *predicate* (сказу́емое).

(1) The subject is any or everything spoken of in the proposition; such, for example, as has been indicated above in § 154, viz. безкоры́стіе, го́рдость, они́.

(2) The predicate is all that speaks of the subject; thus, in the same examples, доброде́тель, поро́къ, бога́ты.

§ 156. The subject and the predicate are sometimes joined by the verb быть, to be, as is seen in the examples given in § 154. The verb быть in the forms of its present tense is, as a rule, omitted; thus, го́рдость поро́къ, pride (is a) vice; я бѣ́денъ,[1] I (am) poor; онъ бога́тъ,[2] he (is) rich.

§ 157. The subject is, generally speaking, a noun in the nominative case. *Ex.* Лѣ́то прошло́,[3] *Summer* has past; Ту́чи закры́ли со́лнце,

---

[1] Abbreviated form of бѣ́дный. *Trans.*
[2] Abbreviated form of бога́тый. *Trans.*
[3] Neuter form of the adjective про́шлый. *Trans.*

*Clouds* hid the sun; &c. Other parts of speech may, however, take the place of a noun substantive as the subject. These are:—(*a*) a noun adjective or a participle: *Ex.* Полѣзное предпочитается прiятному, The *useful* is preferable to the *agreeable*; лѣнивый не замѣчаетъ, что одно *настоящее* принадлежитъ намъ, The *idle* (*man*) does not perceive that the *present* alone belongs to us.—(*b*) Nouns numeral: *Ex.* Тамъ *тысячи* пали за отчизну, There *thousands* fell for fatherland; &c.—(*c*) Pronouns: *Ex.* Я пишу, *I* write; *Этотъ* прилѣженъ а *тотъ* лѣнивъ, *This* one (is) diligent, but *that* one (is) lazy; &c.—(*d*) Verbs in the infinitive mood: *Ex.* Дѣлать другихъ счастливыми есть величайшее счастiе, To *make* others happy is the greatest happiness; &c.—(*e*) Adverbs denoting time and place: Сегодня тепло, It is warm *to-day*; здѣсь весело, а *тамъ* скучно, *Here* (it) is cheerful, but *there* (it) is dull. Adverbs of quantity may also represent the subject: *Ex.* Много погибло и *мало* спаслось, *Many* perished, and *few* were saved.—(*f*) In a few cases interjections: *Ex.* Прогремѣло *ура!* There thundered forth *hurrah!* Раздалось *браво! Bravo* resounded!

§ 158. The predicate may be—(*a*) A noun substantive in the nominative case: *Ex.* Скука есть *болѣзнь* праздныхъ людей, Weariness is the *ailment* of idle people; &c.—(*b*) A noun adjective or a participle, with a shortened termination: *Ex.* Вашъ опекунъ *опытенъ* и *честенъ,* Your guardian (is) *experienced* and *honest;* &c.—(*c*) A verb in the indicative or imperative mood: *Ex.* Онъ *читаетъ,* He *reads;* Помоги вамъ Богъ, God *help* you; &c.—(*d*) An adverb of quality: *Ex.* Жить въ Петербургѣ *приятно,* по очень *дорого,* To live in St. Petersburgh (is) *agreeable,* but very *expensive.*

*Obs.*—In a few cases a pronoun may take the place of the predicate. *Ex.* Я не *ты,* I (am) not *thou;* &c.

§ 159. The subject and the predicate are called the principal parts or elements of the proposition, to which are joined the other and secondary parts that serve to illustrate and amplify the principal parts. The secondary parts consist of the *complement,* the *definition,* and the *circumstantial words.*

§ 160. The complement (дополнительное) illustrates or adds to the signification of the subject and of the predicate. It may be— (*a*) A noun substantive in any of the oblique cases: *Ex.* Онъ любитъ *музыку* и *пѣнiе,* He loves *music* and *singing;* &c.—(*b*) An adjective or a participle when either of these parts of speech stands in the place of a noun substantive : *Ex.* Онъ жалѣетъ *гонимаю* и *слабаю*, He pities the *persecuted* (one) and the *weak;* &c.—(c) A personal pronoun, in any of the oblique cases, and a reflective pronoun : *Ex.* Мы ожидали тебя́, We have expected *thee;* Онъ думаетъ о себѣ, He thinks *of himself.*—(d) A verb in the infinitive mood: *Ex.* Онъ любитъ *читать*, He likes *to read;* &c.

§ 161. The *definition* (опредѣлительное) points to the quality or to any of the attributes, both of the subject and of the predicate, as well as of the complement. The definition may be either an adjective or numeral, or a pronoun (except a personal, relative, and reflective). The definition answers to the question какой? of what kind? чей? whose? который? which? сколько? how much? how many? *Ex.* За всю эту обширную усадьбу *нашъ богатый* сосѣдъ заплатилъ *сто тысячъ* рублей, For *all this vast* farm *our rich* neighbour paid a *hundred thousand* roubles; &c.

§ 162. *Circumstantial words* (обстоятельственныя слова́) are expressed by the various parts of speech in the proposition which indicate *place, time, mode,* and *cause* or *object* of the action :—(a) To indicate the *place* of action the following questions serve : гдѣ? where? куда́? whither? откуда? whence? *Ex.* Онъ былъ въ *Римѣ* и видѣлъ *тамъ* па́пу, He was in *Rome,* and *there* saw the Pope ; &c.—(b) To indicate the *time* of action there are the interrogatives когда́? when? какъ? how? долго-ли? how long? *Ex.* На *праздникахъ* онъ занятъ былъ *каждый день съ утра́ до ве́чера,* During the *holidays* he was occupied *each day from morning till evening.*—(c) To indicate the *mode* of action the questions are какъ ? how ? какимъ образомъ? in what manner? *Ex.* Онъ трудится *неутомимо,* He labours *indefatigably.*—(d) To indicate the *cause* or *object* of the action, the questions are почему́? why? для чего? for what? зачѣмъ? why? отчего? from which cause? *Ex.* Всѣ вооружились *для защиты отечества*, All have armed themselves *for the defence* of fatherland.

> *Obs.*—From the examples here adduced it is apparent that nouns substantive are used in the oblique cases, both as circumstantial words as well as complements. The difference consists in this, that the latter class of words answer to the questions кого? чего? кому? кѣмъ? &c.; whilst the former correspond with the interrogative adverbs гдѣ? куда́? когда́? почему́? &c.

§ 163. Nouns substantive coupled with adjectives, when found separately in the proposition, and serving to illustrate another substantive, are said to be *in apposition. Ex.* Петербургъ, *великолѣпная столица Россіи*, основанъ Петромъ Великимъ, St. Petersburgh, *the magnificent capital of Russia*, (was) founded by Peter the Great; &c.

§ 164. *Appositions* (прпложéніе) likewise have their own complements and definitions, as is apparent from the preceding example: *великолѣпная столица Россіи*.

§ 165 A proper noun, or an appellative noun, may also be used as an apposition. *Ex.* Царь *Іоаннъ*, Tsar *John* ; Рѣка *Амуръ*, River *Amoor* ; &c.

§ 166. *Address* expressed by the vocative case is sometimes found in the beginning, middle, or end of a proposition: *Ex.* Я ожидаю тебя, *любéзный другъ*, I expect thee, *dear friend*. *Introductory* words, such as *Слава Богу*, *Glory to God ; кажется*, *it seems ; можетъ быть*, *perhaps*, &c., are likewise inserted: *Ex.* Вы, *кажется*, устáли, *It seems* you are tired. Neither the *address* nor the *introductory words* enter into the composition of the proposition, and can be omitted without interfering with its sense.

§ 167. The principal parts of the proposition can also be omitted. In that case the subject or the predicate will be understood. *Ex.* Хожу по *полямъ* и *наблюдаю* за работами, *I walk* along the fields and *look after* the works. Here there are expressed the predicates alone, the subject я being in each case understood.

§ 168. With *impersonal* verbs the predicate is in every case expressed without the subject or a person; hence the proposition itself is said to be *impersonal: Ex. Морозитъ*, *it freezes ; вѣрится*, *one believes* ; &c.

§ 169. Propositions, according to their construction, are *simple* or *compound*. A *simple* proposition is confined to one sentence *only*, and consists of but one subject and one predicate: *Ex.* Надéжда *услаждаетъ* жизнь нашу, *Hope charms* our life. A *compound* proposition embraces two or more sentences, and is therefore made up of two or more propositions: *Ex.* Надéжда услаждаетъ жизнь нашу, *мечты украшаютъ* её, а *страсти сокращаютъ*, *Hope charms* our life, *dreams embellish* it, and *passions shorten* (it); &c.

§ 170. Propositions, according to their signification, may be *principal, subordinate,* and *introductory.*

(1) A *principal* proposition comprises some main idea, has its own separate sense, and does not depend on any other proposition: *Ex.* Мой братъ, который недавно произведёнъ въ офицеры, отправился въ походъ, *My brother,* who not long ago was promoted to (be) an officer, *has set out for a campaign;* &c.

(2) A *subordinate* proposition, on the other hand, depends on the principal proposition, which it illustrates, and may be joined both to the subject and to the predicate: not so complements, definitions and circumstantial words. For instance, in the preceding example, the subordinate proposition is joined to the subject. *Subordinate* are coupled with main propositions by means of grammatical parts of speech, viz. relative pronouns, verbs in the form of participles and gerunds, adverbs of time and place, and conjunctions.

(3) An *introductory* proposition is not connected either with a main or subordinate proposition, and may be omitted without upsetting the sense of the passage in which it occurs. *Ex.* Вы, я думаю, скоро кончите дѣло, *You, I think,* will soon finish (your) business. An introductory proposition cannot be placed at the beginning of a sentence: if it is so placed it becomes the principal, and what was the principal is turned into the subordinate proposition; thus, Я думаю что вы скоро кончите дѣло. Here *я думаю* has become the main proposition, and the rest of the sentence has been turned into a subordinate proposition.

§ 171. To a principal or to a subordinate proposition is sometimes joined a *quoted* proposition, comprising some lengthy passage introduced without change: *Ex.* Императоръ Александръ I. сказалъ народу, "Я вступаю не врагомъ а возвращаю вамъ миръ и торговлю," The Emperor Alexander I. said to the people, "I come not as an enemy, but to restore to you peace and commerce."

§ 172. Propositions, according to variety of expression, may be—

(1) *Narrative,* or such as contain the illustration of any sort of subject, or simply a tale concerning it: *Ex.* мечъ былъ нервымъ властелиномъ людей, но одни законы могли быть основаніемъ ихъ гражданскаго счастія, The sword was the first sovereign of the

people, but the laws alone could be the foundation of their civic happiness.

(2) *Interrogative,* or such as suggest questions :—*Ex.* Зачѣ́мъ проходи́мъ мы безъ внима́нія ми́мо трудо́въ земледѣ́льца, проливающаго потъ надъ со́бственною полосо́ю, Why do we pass by without notice the labours of an agriculturist who pours out his sweat over his own strip of land ?

(3) *Exclamatory,* or those which give utterance to a cry of surprise, or of some strong feeling : *Ex.* Два́дцать три милліо́на христіа́нскихъ душъ призыва́ются къ но́вой жи́зни, къ созна́нію своего́ человѣ́ческаго досто́инства ! Twenty-three millions of Christian souls are called to a new life, to the recognition of their own human worth !

(4) *Imperative,* which express a wish, command, or prohibition : *Ex.* Награжда́йте добродѣ́тель, просвѣща́йте люде́й, усовершенствуйте воспита́ніе, *Reward* virtue, *enlighten* the people, *perfect* education.

> *Obs.*—Imperative propositions may be—(a) *impressive,* or those giving expression to a precise injunction. The construction of such entails the addition of the conjunction *же* to the imperative mood : *Ex.* чита́йже гро́мче, read (thou) louder ; &c.—(b) *softening,* or such as are employed in ordinary conversation and in popular phraseology. These are formed by means of the addition of the particle *ка* to the imperative mood : *Ex.* Скажи́ка мнѣ, *Prithee* tell me ; &c.

(5) *Hypothetical* or *conditional,* or such as are formed by the addition of the conjunction *бы* to the past tense of a verb : *Ex.* Когда́ бы вы познако́мились съ нимъ, то полюби́ли бы его, *Had* you become acquainted with him, you *would have* liked him ; &c.

§ 173. *Compound* propositions are formed—

(1) By coupling one principal proposition with another by means of conjunctions. *Ex.* На Бо́га упова́й, *а* самъ не плоша́й, Hope in God, *and* be not careless ; &c.

(2) By coupling *principal* with *subordinate* propositions, by means of the various grammatical parts of speech (*vide* § 170) :

*Ex.* Исто́р*ія* есть па*у́ка*, кото́рая изобража́етъ въ свя́зномъ разска́зѣ суще́ственныя перемѣ́н*ы* въ жи́зни наро́довъ и́ли госуда́рствъ, History is the science which depicts in a connected narrative the actual changes in the life of peoples or of sovereignties. A subordinate proposition may occur at the beginning of a sentence : *Ex. Есл*и *не съумѣешь сказа́ть въ немно́гихъ слова́хъ того́, чѣмъ по́лно се́рдце,* то мно́го-рѣ́чіемъ то́лько разведёшь водо́ю со́бственное чу́вство, *If thou canst not say in a few words that with which (thy) heart (is) full,* then with much speech thou only dilutest thine own feeling with water; &c.

§ 174. Speech is formed by coupling simple or compound propositions possessing some connection of their own.

§ 175. Speech is either *periodical* or *abrupt.—Periodical* speech consists of several compound propositions. *Ex.* Я гото́вился быть свидѣ́телемъ торжества́ великолѣ́пнаго : по торжество́, ви́дѣнное мно́ю превзошло́ моё ожида́ніе. .... Тако́е же чу́вство, како́е потрясло́ мою́ ду́шу, когда́ предста́вились мнѣ въ пе́рвый разъ А́льпы, когда́ и уви́дѣлъ Римъ посреди́ его́ запустѣ́вшей равни́ны, когда́ подходи́лъ ко хра́му Свята́го Петра́, и остановился подъ его́ изуми́тельнымъ сво́домъ. I made myself ready to be a witness of a magnificent triumph : but the triumph which I saw exceeded my expectation. .... The same sort of feeling agitated my mind when the Alps were presented to me for the first time, when I saw Rome amidst her (*lit.* its) desolated ruins, when I came beneath the temple of St. Peter, and remained beneath its amazing vault ; &c.—*Abrupt* speech consists of several simple principal propositions, coupled by grammatical parts of speech. *Ex.* чу́вство уста́лости исче́зло : си́лы мои́ возобнови́лись : дыха́ніе моё ста́ло легко́. The feeling of fatigue disappeared : my strength was renewed : my breathing became easy, &c.

§ 176. Syntax embraces the rules : (1) of the *concord* (согласова́ніе); (2) *government* (управле́ніе); (3) *arrangement* (размѣще́ніе), of words ; and (4) *punctuation* (препина́ніе).

I. CONCORD OF WORDS.

§ 177. Concord of words signifies their regular coupling in all parts of the proposition.

§ 178. The most important rules under this head are the following:— .

(1) The subject and the predicate, when expressed by declinable parts of speech, agree in case, but in gender and number they may differ when the predicate is a noun substantive : *Ex*. Калмы́ки наро́дъ кочу́ющій, The Kalmucks, a nomad *race*, &c.

(2) When the verb быть indicates a temporary condition, the predicate is used in the instrumental case : *Ex*. Бра́тъ мой тогда́ былъ кадетомъ, My brother *was then* a *cadet ;* Пе́рвые бу́дутъ послѣ́дними п послѣ́дніе пе́рвыми, The first *shall be last*, and the last *first ;* &c.

(3) A predicate expressed by a verb or participle with a shortened termination always agrees with the subject in gender, number and person : *Ex*. До́мъ про́данъ, the house has been sold ; дере́вня ку́плена, the village has been bought ; пи́сьма отпра́влены, the letters have beeen despatched ; &c.

(4) Definitions agree with those words which they define in gender, number and case : *Ex*. мно́гіе ди́кіе наро́ды поклоня́ются небе́снымъ свѣти́ламъ, many wild races worship the heavenly luminaries ; &c.

(5) An apposition agrees with its substantive in case, whilst it may differ from it in gender and number : *Ex*. Желѣ́зо, полѣ́знѣ́йшій мета́ллъ, нахо́дится у насъ въ изоби́лій, Iron, a most useful metal, is found with us in great abundance ; &c.

(6) When there are two nouns (an *appellative* and a *proper*) in apposition signifying one and the same object, but of a different gender and number, the predicate agrees as to these with the appellative noun : *Ex*. Го́родъ Аѳи́ны сла́вился въ дре́вности, The town of Athens was famous in antiquity ; &c.

(7) In the case of titles, such as Вели́чество Majesty, Высо́чество Highness, Свѣ́тлость Serene Highness, &c., the words defined by them agree with them in gender : *Ex*. Импера́торское Вели́чество, Imperial Majesty ; Ва́ша Свѣ́тлость, Your Serene Highness, &c. ;—but the predicates belonging to them agree in gender with the personage to whom the title relates : *Ex*. Его́ Импера́торское Вели́чество изво́лилъ возврати́ться изъ Москвы́, His Imperial Majesty was pleased to return from Moscow ; Ей Короле́вское Высо́чество посѣ-

щáла всѣ вы́сшія учéбныя заведéнія, Her Royal Highness visited all the high schools; Егó Свѣ́тлость былъ зáнятъ цѣ́лый деньбъ вáжными дѣлáми, His Serene Highness was engaged the whole day with important business; &c.

(8) If there are two or more substantives of different genders, and one of these is of the masculine gender, the definition will also be of the masculine gender: *Ex.* Онъ принéсъ вамъ *нóвые* плáны, кни́ги и ландкáрты, *кýпленные* по вáшему желáнію, He brought you the *new* plans, books and maps *bought* according to your desire.

(9) If two or more definitions relate to the same object, then both the subject and the predicate are put in the plural number: *Ex.* Бѣ́лое и Азóвское *моря́ нахóдятся* въ предѣ́лахъ Россíи, The White *Sea* and the *Sea* of Azoff *are situated* in the confines of Russia; &c.

(10) When several objects are referred to, and their general number is expressed by the pronouns *всё* or *ничтó*, the predicate is placed in the *singular* number: *Ex.* Всё емý нрáвилось, всё восхищáло егó, *everything pleased, everything charmed* him; Ни прóсьбы, ни мóльбы, ни слёзы несчáстныхъ — *ничтó не моглó* егó трóнуть, Neither the requests nor the prayers nor the tears of the unfortunate—*nothing could touch* him.

(11) A separate object relating to any of *two or more* persons spoken of in the proposition is placed in the singular instead of the plural number: *Ex.* Пóслѣ такóй неудáчи, óба брáта повѣ́сили *носъ* (not носы́), After such misfortune, both brothers became discouraged (*lit.*, hung down their *noses*); &c.

(12) The verb *быть* in the present tense does not always agree with the subject in number, and is sometimes placed in the singular, although the subject be in the plural number: *Ex.* У меня́ есть рѣ́дкія картúны, I have rare pictures, &c.

(13) When the verb *быть* in the past tense is found between two substantives of different genders, it must agree in gender with the first, and not with the second. *Ex.* Пéтръ *былъ* рѣ́звое и весёлое дитя́, Peter *was* a playful and merry child.

(14) When the subject is represented by the adverbs of quantity—мнóго, much, many; мáло, little; нѣ́сколько, some, several; скóлько, how much, how many; стóлько, so much, so

many—the predicate is placed in the neuter gender and singular number. *Ex.* Въ этомъ сраженіи *убито нѣсколько офицеровъ,* In this engagement *several* officers (were) *killed.*

(15) The words мпожество, multitude, бо́льшая часть, greater part, ма́лая часть, lesser part, require the verb or predicate to be in the singular number : *Ex.* Тамъ *собра́лось мно́жество солда́тъ,* There were *collected* a *multitude* of soldiers ; *Бо́льшая часть* на́шихъ товарищей *произведена́* въ офицеры, *The greater part* of our comrades were *promoted* to officers.

(16) Verbs which relate to one object must be put in the same tense and aspect: *Ex.* Онъ *сѣлъ* за столъ, *подумалъ, написа́лъ* рѣши́тельный отвѣтъ и *отпра́вилъ* его къ проси́телю, He *sat down* at the table, *thought a little, wrote* a decisive answer, and *sent* it *off* to the petitioner ;—but when there are adverbs or conjunctions with the verbs, different aspects may be used : *Ex.* Онъ *сѣлъ* за столъ, *до́лго ду́малъ, пото́мъ сталъ писать* отвѣтъ и *наконе́цъ отпра́вилъ* его къ проси́телю, He *sat down* at the table, thought for *a long time,* then *began to write* an answer, and *finally despatched* it to the petitioner.

(17) A gerund in a subordinate, and a verb in a main, proposition must express the action of one and the same person : *Ex.* Получи́въ письмо́, я написа́лъ отвѣтъ, On receiving the letter, I wrote the answer, &c. Therefore it would be irregular to say, Стоя́ на горѣ, глаза́ мои́ восхища́лись прекра́снымъ ви́домъ, Standing on the mountain, my eyes were enchanted with the beautiful sight,—instead of Стоя́ на горѣ, я восхища́лся прекра́снымъ ви́домъ, Stand on the mountain, I was enchanted with the beautiful sight ; &c.

## II. THE GOVERNMENT OF WORDS.

§ 179. In the government of words are explained the various relations between the principal and the secondary parts of the proposition.

§ 180. These relations show the dependence of one word on another, and such words are said to be *governing,* and *governed* or *subordinate : Ex.* Шумъ бу́ри, образова́ніе се́рдца, &c. ; the noise of the tempest, the formation of the heart, &c. Here the words *шумъ* and *образова́ніе* are the governing words, whilst *бу́ри* and *се́рдца* are the governed words, or those dependent thereon.

§ 181. The principal rules in the government of words are contained in the subjoined use of the oblique cases with and without prepositions. The nominative and vocative cases being *direct*, do not depend on other words, and therefore are not subject to government.

(a.) *Use of the Cases without Prepositions.*

§ 182. The genitive case answers to the questions, кого? of whom? чего? of what? чей? чья? чье? whose? and is used—

(1) Where there are two nouns substantive in a complementary phrase: *Ex.* Меня изумила высота *горъ*, The height of the mountains astonished me; &c. A complement is sometimes used in the dative instead of in the genitive case: *Ex.* Здѣсь назначена цѣна *мѣстамъ*, Here (is) noted the prices *to the places;* &c. In certain masculine nouns signifying quantity, the termination of the genitive case is changed into that of the dative: *Ex.* Я купилъ пудъ *сахару* и фунтъ *чаю*, I bought a pood (36 lbs.) of *sugar* and a pound of *tea* (*vide* § 39). Nouns substantive in the genitive case can be changed into nouns adjective: *Ex.* Лучъ со́лнца, A ray of sun; *солнечный* лучъ, *solar* ray; &c.

(2) In the case of nouns substantive derived from active verbs which require the accusative case: *Ex.* Чтеніе полезныхъ книгъ способствуетъ къ *образованію ума*, The *reading of useful books* aids in the *education of the understanding;* &c. Certain nouns derived from neuter verbs also require the genitive case: *Ex.* Въ минеральныхъ источникахъ происходитъ кипѣніе *воды*, In mineral sources the *boiling of water* takes place; &c.

(3) In indications of *quantity, measure*, and *weight: Ex.* У насъ много работы а мало времени, We have *much work*, but *little time.*

(4) After nouns adjective of the comparative degree: *Ex.* Старый другъ лучше новыхъ двухъ, An old friend (is) better than *two new ones*; &c.

(5) In the case of nouns adjective indicating *merit, strangeness, fullness: Ex.* Достойный уваженія, *worthy of respect;* чуждый гордости, *free from pride;* онъ получилъ кошелёкъ полный *денегъ*, He received a purse *full of money.*

(6) In the case of the numerals полтора, два, оба, три, четыре, and their compounds, such as двадцать два, сорокъ три, &c., the genitive case is placed in the singular number: *Ex.* полтора *рубля*,

1½ *roubles;* два *стола́,* two *tables;* о́ба *бра́та,* both *brothers;* три кни́ги, three *books;* четы́ре *стекла́,* four *panes of glass;* пять-десять три *солда́та,* fifty-three *soldiers,* &c.; but with all the other numerals the genitive case plural is used: *Ex.* Пять столо́въ, во́семь бра́тьевъ, сто стёколъ, ты́сяча книгъ, five *tables,* eight *brothers,* 100 *panes of glass,* 1000 *books,* &c.

(7) In the case of the numerals два, о́ба, три, четы́ре, and their compounds, the adjective is used in the nominative case of the plural number, and in the same gender as that to which the substantive in question belongs: *Ex.* Его́ *три послѣ́днія сочине́нія* имѣ́ли большо́й успѣ́хъ, His *three last compositions* had a great success; &c. In the case of all the other numerals, beginning with five, the adjective and the substantive must agree in number and case: *Ex.* Семь послѣ́днихъ сочине́ній, the seven last compositions; &c.

(8) In the case of active verbs, when their action extends to a part only of the object: *Ex.* Дай мнѣ *де́негъ,* Give me *some money.* With such verbs are always understood adverbs of quantity, such as *немно́го, little, few;* нѣ́сколько, *some, several;* &c.

(9) In the case of active verbs with the negative adverb *не, not: Ex.* Я не люблю́ пра́здности, I do *not* like idleness; &c. The genitive case is also used when the negative precedes the verb which comes before the governing verb: *Ex.* Ты не хотѣ́лъ читать э́той кни́ги, Thou didst *not* desire to read *this book.*

(10) Active, reflective, and common verbs implying *wish, expectation, deprivation, fear, danger,* require the genitive case: *Ex.* Я желаю вамъ успѣ́ха въ ва́шемъ дѣ́лѣ, I *wish* you *success* in your business; Онъ до́лго жда́лъ награ́ды, He long *expected* a *reward;* Вы лиши́ли меня́ удово́льствія ви́дѣть васъ, You have *deprived* me of the *satisfaction* of seeing (*lit.* to see) you; Я опаса́юсь пожа́ра а ты бои́шся наводне́нія, I *dread* a *fire,* and thou *fearest* an *inundation;* &c.

(11) The following verbs also govern the genitive case:— требовать, to require; достига́ть, to attain; сто́ить, to cost; отвѣ́дывать, to test; домога́ться, to solicit; слу́шаться, to obey; стыди́ться, to be ashamed of; and certain others of similar signification, which answer to the questions кого́? чего́?

(12) The genitive case is required after adverbs denoting *place,* such as во́злѣ, beside; по́длѣ, near; близъ, near; вдоль, along;

внѣ, outside; внутри́, inside; снару́жи, on the outside; ми́мо, by; о́коло, near; and others after which are put the questions кого́? чего́?

§ 183. The dative case answers to the questions кому́? чему́? and is used—

(1) With certain active verbs, such as подража́ть, to copy; помо́чь, to aid; служи́ть, to serve; угожда́ть, to please; повреди́ть, to harm; сопу́тствовать, to travel with; &c.

(2) With certain reflective and common verbs, such as удивля́ться, to be surprised at; ра́доваться, to rejoice at; преда́ться, to give one's self up to; моли́ться, to worship; жа́ловаться, to complain to; нра́виться, to please; &c.

(3) With the impersonal verbs, such as жаль, it is a pity; сты́дно, it is shameful; хо́чется, one desires; на́добно, it is necessary; ну́жно, it is needful; &c.

(4) When the complement is a personal object indicating *relationship, friendship, enmity*, &c.: *Ex.* Онъ мнѣ дя́дя, ты ему́ другъ, He (is) *uncle to me,* thou (art a) *friend to him;* Онъ Петру́ большо́й непрія́тель, He is a *great enemy to Peter;* &c.

(5) With the adverbs прили́чно, becoming; соотвѣ́тственно, corresponding to; сообра́зно, conformably to; &c.

(6) The following adverbs likewise require the dative case. вопреки́, contrary to; на-зло́, despite; на́-смѣхъ, in derision of; на-переко́ръ, in spite of; въ-уго́ду, for the pleasure of; &c.

§ 184. The accusative case answers to the questions кого́? что? and is used—

(1) As a complement, after active verbs without a negative: *Ex.* Онъ купи́лъ рѣ́дкую кни́гу, He *bought a rare book;* &c.

(2) As a complement, after neuter verbs indicating a known *distance* or *time: Ex.* Онъ бѣжа́лъ цѣ́лую вёрсту, He ran *a whole verst;* мы не спа́ли всю ночь, We did not sleep the *whole night;* &c.

§ 185. The instrumental case answers to the questions кѣмъ? чѣмъ? and is used—

(1) With all the passive verbs: *Ex.* Онъ былъ люби́мъ всѣ́ми това́рищами, He was beloved by all his comrades; &c.

(2) With the reciprocal verbs, followed by the preposition съ: *Ex.* Нáши вóйска хрáбро сражáлись съ непріятелями, Our troops bravely engaged *with* the enemy; &c.

(3) With certain of the reflective and the common verbs, such as занимáться, to occupy one's self; умыться, to wash one's self; гордиться, to pride one's self; восхищáтся, to be charmed with; любовáться, to delight in; &c.

(4) With verbs indicating *power, management, arrangement*, such as владѣть, to rule; управлять, to govern; распоряжáться, to dispose; завѣдывать, to manage; обладáть, to possess; располагáть, to place; &c.

(5) The following verbs likewise require the instrumental case: дорожить, to prize; жертвовáть, to sacrifice; обиловать, to abound in; страдáть, to suffer; &c.

(6) Nouns substantive derived from verbs which govern the instrumental case require that the words subordinate to them should also be in the same case: *Ex.* распоряжéніе *имýществомъ*, the distribution *of property;* завѣдывáніе *дѣлáми*, the management *of affairs;* &c.

§ 186. The prepositional case is always used with prepositions. With the prepositional case are used many verbs answering to the questions о комъ? о чёмъ? въ чёмъ? при чёмъ? such as дýмать, to think about; мечтáть, to reflect; сожалѣть, to regret; печáлиться, to grieve; забóтиться, to busy one's self; хлопотáть, to bustle; упражняться, to occupy one's self; находиться, to be situated; состоять, to consist of; &c.

§ 187. Certain verbs require various cases. The more frequently used of such are the following:—

(1) жалѣть, to pity; просить, to beg; which require the genitive or the prepositional.

(2) удовлетворять, to satisfy; покровительствовать, to protect; which require the dative and the accusative. The dative when the action relates to an intellectual object: *Ex.* удовлетворять *желáнію, любопытству*, to satisfy *desire, curiosity;* покровительствовать *наýкамъ* и *худóжествамъ*, to encourage *the sciences* and *arts.* The accusative with a personal object: *Ex.* удовлетворить *просителя*, to satisfy the *petitioner;* покровительствовать *бѣдныхъ сиротъ*, to protect *poor orphans*, &c.

(3) In the case of the verbs учи́ть, to teach, and обуча́ть, to train, the personal noun is placed in the accusative, and the object of the action in the dative, case: *Ex.* Онъ у́читъ *мою́ сестру́ му́зыкѣ*, He teaches *my sister music*, &c.

(4) The verb слѣ́довать, to follow, governs the dative and the instrumental. The former, where intellectual nouns are concerned: *Ex.* Слѣ́довать *до́брымъ примѣ́рамъ и совѣ́тамъ*, To follow *good examples* and *counsels*. It requires all other nouns to be in the instrumental case, before which is used the preposition *за*: *Ex.* во́ины слѣ́дуютъ *за свои́мъ полково́дцемъ*, The soldiers *follow (after) their leader*, &c.

(5) The verbs испра́шивать, to ask for, заслу́живать, to deserve, иска́ть, to seek, when used in the present tense, and in the imperfect aspect of the past and future tenses, require the genitive case; but when used in the perfect aspect they govern the accusative case: *Ex.* Онъ испра́шиваетъ, *or* испра́шивалъ, *ва́шего согла́сія*, He asks, *or* he asked, for *your consent;* Онъ испроси́лъ, *or* испро́ситъ, *ва́ше согла́сіе*, He asked, *or* will ask, for *your consent;* &c.

(6) The following verbs govern the accusative and the instrumental cases:—пренебрега́ть, to despise; броса́ть, to throw; вертѣ́ть, to turn; промышля́ть, to deal; торгова́ть, to trade; бры́згать, to sprinkle.

(7) The verb удосто́ивать, which requires the genitive case, sometimes governs the instrumental case also: *Ex.* удосто́ить *награ́ды и ми́лости*, to bestow *rewards* and *favours;* Госуда́рь удосто́илъ его́ *свои́мъ разгово́ромъ*, The sovereign honoured him *with his conversation;* &c.

(8) The verb наблюда́ть, to observe, when it suggests the question что?, requires the accusative case: *Ex.* наблюда́ть *поря́докъ и чистоту́*, to observe *order* and *cleanliness;* and when it suggests the questions за чѣмъ? за кѣмъ? it takes the instrumental case, with the preposition *за*: *Ex.* наблюда́ть *за поря́дкомъ и за чистото́ю*, to look *after order* and *cleanliness.*

*Obs.*—The rules of government, to which a verb is subject, remain the same when that verb is changed into another part of speech: *Ex.* Онъ дости́гъ свое́й *цѣ́ли*, He attained his *object;* достига́ющій *цѣ́ли*, one who attains (his) *object;* достиже́ніе *цѣ́ли*, the attainment of an *object;* &c. But nouns substantive, derived from active verbs which require the accusative case, govern the genitive, as already stated in § 182: *Ex.* строе́ніе до́ма, чте́ніе кни́ги, the building *of the house*, the reading *of the book*. Others, again, govern the dative, with the preposition къ: *Ex.* почте́ніе къ *роди́телямъ*, уваже́ніе къ *ста́ршимъ*, reverence *to parents*, respect *to elders*; &c.

(9) The verb благодари́ть requires the accusative case, whilst words derived from it govern the dative: *Ex.* Я благодарю́ *Бо́га*, I thank *God*; благодаре́ніе *Бо́гу*, thanks to *God*; благодаря́ *своему́ дя́дѣ*, онъ уплати́лъ всѣ долги́, thanks to *his uncle*, he paid all his debts.

(b) *Use of the Cases with Prepositions.*

§ 188. The government of the oblique cases likewise depends on prepositions:—

(1) The prepositions безъ, для, ра́ди, до, изъ, отъ, у, and their compounds изъ за, изъ-подъ, always require the genitive case.

(2) Къ (ко) governs the dative case.

(3) Про, чрезъ (че́резъ), сквозь, the accusative.

(4) Надъ, the instrumental.

(5) При, the prepositional.

(6) The prepositional adverb ме́жду (межъ) requires the genitive and the instrumental: *Ex.* Этотъ го́родъ лежи́тъ *ме́жду двухъ рѣкъ*, or *ме́жду двумя́ рѣка́ми*, This town lies *between two rivers*; &c.

(7) When за answers to the question куда́? whither? it requires the accusative: *Ex.* за рѣку́, за́ море, beyond the river, beyond the sea. But when it answers to the question гдѣ? where? it governs the instrumental: *Ex.* за рѣко́ю, за́ моремъ. Likewise, when it answers to the question за что? for what? it requires the accusative case: *Ex.* Ты былъ нака́занъ *за лѣность*, а онъ получи́лъ награ́ду *за прилежа́ніе*, Thou wast punished *for idleness*, and he received a reward *for industry*.

(8) When подъ answers to the question куда́? whither? it requires the accusative: *Ex.* Онъ сѣлъ *подъ де́рево*, He took a seat *under the tree*. But when it answers to the question гдѣ? where?

it governs the instrumental : *Ex.* онъ сидитъ подъ *деревомъ,* he is sitting *under the tree.*

(9) Предъ or передъ requires both the accusative and the instrumental : *Ex.* Онъ предсталъ предъ Государя or предъ Государемъ, He presented himself *before the sovereign.* With inanimate and abstract objects, this preposition is more often used in the instrumental case: *Ex.* Онъ явился предъ городомъ, He appeared *before the town ;* Онъ правъ предъ своею совѣстью, He (is) right *in his own conscience;* &c.

(10) When въ (во) answers to the question куда? whither? it requires the accusative : *Ex.* Онъ пошёлъ въ *поле,* He went *into the field.* But when it answers to the question гдѣ? where? it governs the prepositional : *Ex.* Онъ гуляетъ въ *полѣ,* he takes a walk *in the field.* The preposition въ (во) with certain verbs indicating *promotion, bestowal of rank or reward,* under any conditions whatever, requires the accusative case of the plural number, and that case must in such instances be like the nominative : *Ex.* Произвесть въ офицеры, to promote to (be an) officer ; назначить въ кандидаты, to appoint (as) candidate ; &c.

(11) When на answers to the questions куда? whither? на кого? on whom ? на что? on what? it requires the accusative case : *Ex.* Онъ отправился на островъ, He set out *for* the island ; Я надѣюсь на вашу дружбу, I rely *on* your friendship. But when the same preposition answers to the questions гдѣ? where? на комъ? on whom? на чемъ? on what (implying rest) ? it governs the prepositional : *Ex.* Гора Этна находится на островѣ Сициліи, Mount Etna is situated in (*lit.* on) the island of Sicily ; &c.

(12) When о (объ) answers to the questions о что *or* обо что ? against what? it requires the accusative : *Ex.* Онъ ушибся о камень, He hurt himself *against* the stone. But when it answers to the questions о комъ? about whom ? о чёмъ? about what ? it governs the prepositional case : *Ex.* Онъ говоритъ о камнѣ, He speaks *about* the stone ; &c.

(13) When съ (со) answers to the question съ чего? from off what? it requires the genitive case : *Ex.* Онъ упалъ съ лошади, He fell from off the horse. When it answers to the question съ кого? like whom ? со что? like what? indicating comparison, it requires the accusative : *Ex.* Величиною съ лошадь, In size *like a* horse ? &c. When, again, it answers to the questions съ кѣмъ ? with whom ? съ

чѣмъ? with what? it governs the instrumental: *Ex.* Онъ купи́лъ са́ни съ ло́шадью, He bought a sledge *with* a horse; &c.

(14) When *no* answers to the questions по чему́? over what? and по чёмъ? at what rate? it requires the dative case: *Ex.* Онъ гуля́етъ по́ полу, He walks *on* the floor; Я плачу́ по рублю́, I pay *at the rate of* a rouble. But when it answers to the question по что? *up to* what? it governs the accusative: *Ex.* Онъ ушёлъ въ во́ду по са́мую ше́ю, He went into the water *up to* (his) very neck. When, again, this preposition answers to the question по комъ? after whom? it governs the prepositional: *Ex.* Онъ пла́четъ по отцѣ, He cries *after* (his) father. When *no* is used in the sense of по́слѣ, after, it likewise takes the prepositional case: *Ex.* По сме́рти Петра́ Вели́каго, *After* the death of Peter the Great; &c.

### III. THE PLACING OF WORDS.

§ 189. The placing or arrangement of words shows the order in which they should follow when used in speech.

§ 190. In the arrangement of words in a proposition, that order must infallibly be adhered to in which our thoughts succeed each other. The more closely we keep to the ordinary conversational style in the arrangement of our words, the more natural, easy, and clear, will be our expressions.

§ 191. This very style, the use of which is maintained by cultivated writers, comprises the observance of the following most important rules:—

(1) The principal object in our sentence should be placed first of all, *i.e.* first should come the *subject,* then the *action* of the subject, or the *predicate,* and lastly the *complement: Ex.* Пётръ основа́лъ Петербургъ, Peter founded St. Petersburg; &c. Speech should begin with those words which most occupy our thoughts: *Ex.* Гря́нулъ си́льный громъ, *Rumbled* the loud thunder; &c.

(2) Sometimes before the principal portion of the proposition the secondary parts are placed, as these serve to prepare the way for the main object of the narrative: *Ex.* Въ тѣни́ высо́кой ли́пы, на берегу́ Москвы́ рѣки́, лежа́ли на травѣ два молоды́е человѣ́ка, *In the shade of a tall lime tree, on the bank of the river Moscow,* two young men lay on the grass.

(3) Where there are many definitions placed together, the following order should be observed: first the *pronoun,* then the

*numeral*, after these the *adjective or participle*, and last of all the *noun substantive*: *Ex*. Тѣ два бѣдные брата имѣютъ хорошія способности, Those two poor brothers have good abilities; &c.

(4) A *qualifying* noun adjective is always placed before a *possessive* adjective: *Ex*. Богатая золотая шпага, a *rich* golden sword. And *circumstantial* adjectives are placed before both qualifying and possessive adjectives: *Ex*. Здѣшнее пріятное общество, the *local* pleasant society; &c.

(5) *Cardinal* numerals are placed before a noun substantive: *Ex*. Ему отъ роду семьдесятъ лѣтъ, He is *seventy* years old. To merely express a number *approximately*, the numeral may be placed after the substantive: *Ex*. Ему отъ роду лѣтъ семьдесятъ, He is *about seventy* years old.

(6) *Ordinal* numerals are placed before cardinal: *Ex*. Первые два часа, the *first* two hours.

(7) From the juxta-position of cases similar in termination an irregularity, and even a confusion of expression, ensues: *Ex*. Онъ почитался всѣмъ войскомъ опытнымъ и храбрымъ полководцемъ, He was considered *by* all the troops an experienced and brave leader. In order to avoid such a fault, the words must either be transposed or their cases changed: *Ex*. Онъ почитался во всёмъ войскѣ опытнымъ и храбрымъ полководцемъ, He was considered *in* the whole army, &c.

(8) Verbs should not be placed at the end of the proposition: *Ex*. Онъ разныя науки знаетъ, He *knows* various sciences. Instead of this, the sentence should stand thus, Онъ знаетъ, &c., He *knows*, &c. This rule may only be departed from when the whole emphasis of the phrase is contained in the verb: *Ex*. Добрыхъ людей хвалятъ, а злыхъ *презираютъ*, Good people are *praised*, but wicked (people) are *despised*; &c.

(9) Adverbs of *quality* are placed before a verb when a complement or a subordinate proposition is attached to it: *Ex*. Крыловъ отлично писалъ басни, которыя, безъ сомнѣнія, вы читали нѣсколько разъ, Krwiloff wrote fables excellently, which doubtless you have read several times. But when the verb is unaccompanied by a complement, adverbs may be placed after it: *Ex*. Крыловъ писалъ *отлично*, Krwiloff wrote *excellently*.

(10) An adverb must infallibly be placed before that word which it qualifies: *Ex*. Онъ совершенно кончилъ новый переводъ, He has *completely* finished (his) new translation, &c. If this rule is not

observed, and if the adverb is transposed, an altogether contrary signification will result : *Ex.* Онъ кончилъ *совершенно* новый переводъ, He has finished (his) *perfectly* new translation.

(11) The negative adverb *не* must be placed before that word to which the negation refers : *Ex.* Онъ *не* сегодня былъ у брата а вчера, He was *not* at (his) brother's to-day, but yesterday. The following arrangement would therefore be irregular : Онъ *не* былъ сегодня у брата а вчера. A similar rule must be observed with all words used in the sense of adverbs. Such should infallibly be placed before the words to which they relate : *Ex.* Извѣстите меня, по-крайней мѣрѣ, о здоровьѣ вашемъ, Inform me, at least, about your health. This sentence would have a directly contrary signification were it to be thus written : извѣстите, по крайней мѣрѣ, меня, &c., Inform *me at least*, &c.

(12) In the construction of conditional or prepositional propositions with impersonal verbs, or with adverbs, to the conjunction *бы* is added the past tense of the verb *быть* : *Ex.* Вамъ полезно было бы прогуливаться, *It would have been* useful to you to take an airing. Many offend against this rule by expressing the phrase thus : Вамъ *полезно бы* прогуливаться.

(13) The conjunction *бы* must not be used in one and the same proposition : *Ex.* Если бы я такъ коротко не зналъ бы васъ, то не повѣрилъ бы вамъ, If I *had* not so intimately known you, I *would not have* believed you. Here the conjunction *бы* should only be inserted in the first proposition, after the word *если*.

(14) One and the same word should not be often repeated, especially if that word be a pronoun : *Ex.* Онъ выкупилъ *ихъ*, взялъ *ихъ* къ себѣ, кормилъ *ихъ* какъ *своихъ* дѣтей, и отослалъ *ихъ* къ родителямъ *ихъ*, He bought *them*, took *them* to himself, as *his own* children, and sent *them* away to *their* parents.

(15) Words, the signification of which is contained in the preceding word, must not be repeated : *Ex.* Сегодняшній день наша работа *долго продолжалась*, To-day's day our work *was long continued*,—should be Сегодня наша работа была продолжительна, To-day our work, &c. Such a fault is called a *pleonasm*.

(16) Expressions should not be turned in a way that is foreign to the Russian language : *Ex.* Вы слишкомъ еще молоды, чтобы занять столь важную должность, You are still too young to undertake such an important duty. Such turnings of phrase appertain to the

French language. In Russian they should be expressed thus: вы ещё такъ мо́лоды, что не мо́жете запи́ть, &c. An error of this kind is called a *gallicism*.

### IV. Punctuation.

§ 192. The signs of punctuation serve to illustrate the coupling or disconnecting of propositions and their parts.

§ 193. *The signs of punctuation* (знакъ препинанія) are:—
(1) *comma*, запятая (,) — (2) *semicolon*, то́чка съ запято́й (;) — (3) *colon*, двоето́чіе (:) — (4) *full stop*, то́чка (.) — (5) *point of suspension*, многото́чіе (.....) — (6) *note of admiration*, знакъ восклица́тельный (!) — (7) *note of interrogation*, знакъ вопроси́тельный (?) — (8) *hyphen*, черта́ or тире́ (-) — (9) *parenthesis*, ско́бка or знакъ вмѣсти́тельный ( ) — (10) *inverted commas*, двузапята́я or вно́сный знакъ (" ").

§ 194. The *comma* is placed—

(1) Between two or more subjects and predicates which are not connected by conjunctions: *Ex.* Везу́вій, Этна и Ге́кла суть огнедышащія го́ры въ Евро́пѣ, Vesuvius, Etna and Hecla are the volcanic mountains of (*lit.* in) Europe; &c.

(2) When the following conjunctions are repeated, *и, ни, или*: *Ex.* И дождь и снѣгъ, шли, *Both* rain *and* snow fell, &c.; Онъ не умѣетъ ни читать, ни писать, He can *neither* read *nor* write; Вы или не могли, или не хотѣли этого сдѣлать, You *either* could not, *or* did not wish, to do this.

(3) When the conjunction *и* couples the main propositions with the various subjects: *Ex.* Въ тотъ день разрази́лась ужа́сная бу́ря, и проливно́й дождь затопи́лъ мно́гія у́лицы, On that day broke a terrible storm, *and* heavy rain flooded many streets. But when the conjunction *и* couples two principal propositions which relate to one and the same subject, the comma is not inserted: *Ex.* Тамъ свирѣпствовала си́льная бу́ря и производи́ла стра́шныя опустоше́нія, There a violent storm raged *and* produced frightful desolation.

(4) A comma is placed before the conjunction *и* when the latter of two propositions comprises the *result of the first*, and when after the conjunction *и* are understood the conjunctions потому́, оттого́: *Ex.* Я сего́дня много ходи́лъ, и (*оттого*) уста́лъ, I have walked much to-day, *and* (*hence*) I am tired, &c.

(5) If for the conjunction *и* the conjunctions какъ и, такъ и, can

be substituted, then a comma is not placed before и : *Ex.* Труды доставили ему *и* славу *и* состояніе, (His) labours brought him *both* fame *and* fortune,—instead of *какъ* славу, *такъ и* состояніе.

(6) Before the conjunction *или*, when it signifies explanation : *Ex.* Гельвеція, *или* Швейцарія страна гористая, Helvetia *or* Switzerland (is a) mountainous country. But when *или* is used in a disjunctive sense, the comma is not used : *Ex.* Онъ желалъ бы ѣхать въ Германію *или* Италію, He wished that he might go to Germany *or* to Italy.

(7) In short propositions before the conjunctions *a* and *но* : *Ex.* Онъ приходилъ къ вамъ, *но* вы уже уѣхали, He came to you, *but* you had already gone away ; &c.

(8) With two or more qualifying adjectives without conjunctions : *Ex.* Свеаборгъ есть *твёрдая, грозная,* и *неприступная* крѣпость, Sveaborg is a *solid, imposing,* and *impregnable* fortress. But when one of the adjectives is a *possessive* or *circumstantial* adjective, the comma is not inserted : *Ex.* Вчерашній пріятный вечеръ, *Yesterday's pleasant* evening.

(9) Between commas are placed all the annexes of the subject and of the predicate, as also the subordinate and introductory propositions and words : *Ex.* Вашъ трудъ, *кажется,* приходитъ къ концу, Your labour, *it seems,* approaches the end.

> *Obs.* 1.—Participles, gerunds, the pronouns который, кой, какой, кто, что, the adverbs какъ-то, то-есть, напримѣръ, кромѣ, and the conjunctions что, будто, если, то, нежели-чѣмъ, кромѣ, какъ, require a comma to be placed before them, as also words which separate the subordinate from the main proposition. If, however, a participle is employed as an adjective, and a gerund as an adverb, a comma is not inserted : *Ex.* Человѣкъ *трудящійся* не знаетъ скуки, The man *who labours* does not know dullness ; Онъ читаетъ *стоя,* He reads (whilst) *standing.*
>
> *Obs.* 2.—The *subject*, the *predicate,* and the *copula,* are not separated by signs of punctuation : *Ex.* Алпы покрыты снѣгомъ, The Alps (are) covered with snow, &c. Neither are definitions or complements divided from their principal parts : *Ex.* Вершины многихъ Алпійскихъ горъ покрыты вѣчнымъ снѣгомъ и льдомъ, The summits of many Alpine mountains (are) covered with perpetual snow and ice.

(10) The adverbs во-пéрвыхъ, во-вторы́хъ, &c., and the conjunction наконéцъ, are separated by commas: *Ex*. *Во-пéрвыхъ*, вы издéржите тутъ мнóго дéнегъ, а *во-вторы́хъ*, потеря́ете мнóго врéмени, *Firstly* you there spend much money, and *secondly* you lose much time; Наконéцъ, онъ рѣши́лся ѣхать въ деревню, *At last* he decided to ride to the village.

(11) If nouns in the vocative case are found in the middle of a sentence, they are separated by commas: *Ex*. Къ вамъ, *ми́лостивый госудáрь*, обраща́юсь съ прóсьбою, To you, *dear sir*, I turn with a request. But when a sentence begins or ends with a noun in the vocative case, after that noun notes of admiration will be put: *Ex*. *Ми́лостивый Госудáрь!* позвóльте обрати́ться къ вамъ, &c., *Dear sir!* allow me to turn towards you, &c.

§ 195. A *semicolon* divides one proposition from another:—

(1) When its several parts have been already separated by commas: *Ex*. Толпы́ жи́телей бѣжáли изъ огня́, полки́ рýсскіе шли въ огóнь; одни́ спасáли жизнь, другíе несли́ её на жéртву,—Crowds of inhabitants fled from the fire, Russian regiments went into it; some saved their lives, others sacrificed them.

(2) In abrupt speech, when the main propositions are expressed briefly, and do not depend on each other: *Ex*. Продолговáтыми островáми разбрóсаны небольшíя рóщи; отъ деревни до деревни бѣгýтъ ýзкія дорóжки; цéркви бѣлѣютъ,—In (shape like) oblong islands are scattered small groves; from village to village run narrow paths; the churches look white.

§ 196. A *colon* is placed—

(1) In the middle of the proposition, before the explanation of any of the parts or appellations: *Ex*. Человѣкъ имѣетъ пять внѣшнихъ чувствъ: зрѣніе, слухъ, вкусъ, обоня́ніе и осяза́ніе,—Man has five exterior senses: sight, hearing, taste, scent and touch; &c.

(2) Before quoted or foreign words: *Ex*. Рýсская послóвица говори́тъ: "учéнье свѣтъ а неучéнье тьма,"—A Russian proverb says: "learning (is) light, and ignorance (is) darkness."

(3) Before a subordinate proposition, when it comprises in itself the explanation of the causes or results of the action, expressed in the main proposition, and when with this may be placed the conjunction потомý-что: *Ex*. Онъ убѣди́лся въ невозмóжности жить въ

столицѣ : *доходы его уменьшались*, а *расходы увеличивались*,—He convinced himself of the impossibility of living in the capital: his income decreased, and his expenditure increased. This sentence can be thus expressed : потому-что доходы его уменьшались, &c.

§ 197. The *full-stop* is placed—

(1) At the end of the sentence or proposition which comprises in itself complete meaning. (See *Ex.* § 175.)

(2) After separate words not possessed of any grammatical bond. For example, the table of contents of books, or circulars : О правахъ вообще, about rights generally, &c.

(3) With shortened words : *Ex.* Ив. Гончаровъ, Iván Gontchároff, &c.

§ 198. *Points of suspension* are inserted to mark some unexpected interruption of speech : *Ex.* Какое-то предчувствіе меня устрашаетъ .... но, нѣтъ, это мечта ! Some sort of presentiment distresses me ..... but, no, it is a dream !

§ 199. A *note of interrogation* is placed after a question : Кто пришёлъ ? Who has come ? &c.

§ 200. A *note of admiration* is placed wherever a wish, command, prohibition, are indicated, and also after interjections : *Ex.* Исполни скорѣй ! Смирно ! Do (it) quickly ! Silence ! Intense surprise is sometimes indicated by a double note of admiration (!!), and strong doubt by a double note of interrogation (??).

§ 201. A *hyphen* is placed—

(1) Whenever any word has been omitted : *Ex.* Законъ мой—правда, My law (is the) truth ; Богъ-мой щитъ, God (is) my shield.

(2) In the case of some unexpected change of speech : *Ex.* Солнце скрылось—и вдругъ, какъ будто бы изъ глубины ада, заревѣла буря—The sun was hid, and suddenly, as if from the depths of hell, began to roar *the tempest*.

(3) Between the speeches of two persons when they are not named : *Ex.* Чѣмъ ты занимаешся ? Читаю Исторію Карамзина.—Который томъ ? Двѣнадцатый. With what art thou occupied ? I am reading Karamzin's history.—Which volume ? The twelfth.

§ 202. Words or whole illustrative passages are placed within *parentheses*: *Ex.* Монбла́нъ (*бѣлая гора́*) есть высоча́йшая изъ горъ въ Евро́пѣ, Mont Blanc (*the white mountain*) is the highest mountain in Europe, &c.

§ 203. *Inverted commas* are placed in order to distinguish quoted or foreign words that are used in the sentence: *Ex.* Екатери́на Втора́я сказа́ла: "Лу́чше прости́ть де́сять вино́вныхъ чѣмъ наказа́ть одного́ неви́ннаго." Catherine II. said: "It is better to pardon ten criminals than to punish one innocent person." &c.

## THIRD PART.
(Отдѣле́ніе Шре́тіе).

### ORTHOGRAPHY.

§ 204. Orthography treats of the regular use of words in writing.

§ 205. The chief rules of orthography consist in the proper use of letters and of separate words, and in the correct division of syllables.

§ 206. Letters, according to their delineation, are *capitals* (прописна́я) and *linear* (строчна́я).

#### USE OF CAPITALS.

§ 207. Capital letters are written—

(1) At the beginning of each sentence.

(2) After a full stop.

(3) After a colon when inverted commas appear in the proposition: *Ex.* Суво́ровъ отвѣча́лъ: "Я зна́ю Куту́зова, а Куту́зовъ зна́стъ меня́;"—Soovóroff answered: "I know Kootóozoff, and Kootóozoff knows me."

(4) After notes of interrogation and of admiration, if the meaning of the sentence is finished: *Ex.* Ты и́щешь вѣрнаго

счастія? Dost thou seek true happiness? Идёмъ на враговъ! Let us go against the enemy!

(5) At the beginning of every verse.

(6) In nouns relating to the Divinity: *Ex.* Богъ, God; Создатель, Creator; Провидѣніе, Providence; &c.

(7) In the names of Saints: *Ex.* Апостолъ, Apostle; Пророкъ, Prophet; Предтеча, Forerunner; &c.

(8) In Proper Names: *Ex.* Александръ, Alexander; Марья, Mary; Лондонъ, London; Днѣпръ, Dneiper; Везувій, Vesuvius, &c.

(9) In adjectives employed as proper names: *Ex.* Россійская Имперія, Russian Empire; Чёрное Море, Black Sea, &c.

(10) In various words used in the sense of proper nouns; such, for instance, as the names of ships, of streets, of bridges, &c.

(11) The name, patronymic, and title of the ruling Emperor, and of the whole of the most august House are written in full, in capital letters: *Ex.* ЕГО ИМПЕРАТОРСКОЕ ВЕЛИЧЕСТВО ГОСУДАРЬ ИМПЕРАТОРЪ АЛЕКСАНДРЪ АЛЕКСАНДРОВИЧЪ, His Imperial Majesty the Sovereign Emperor Alexander, Son of Alexander, &c. Likewise the adjectives which refer to the Sovereign: *Ex.* ВЫСОЧАЙШІЙ, Most High, &c.

> *Obs.*—The initial letters only of the names and titles of foreign ruling personages are written with capital letters: *Ex.* Его Императорское и королевское Величество Императоръ Германскій и Король Прусскій Вильгельмъ, His Imperial and Kingly Majesty the German Emperor and Prussian King William, &c.

(12) In pronouns relating to the person of the Emperor and of his House: *Ex.* ЕГО ВЕЛИЧЕСТВО, во время пребыванія Своего въ Царскомъ Селѣ, повелѣлъ доставить къ Нему отчёты, His Majesty, during his stay at the Royal village, ordered (them) to send reports to him, &c.

(13) In letters and business papers all titles—like князь, prince; графъ, count; баронъ, baron—ranks, names, and offices, when a person is indicated by such: *Ex.* Генералъ Фельдмаршалъ Князь Барятинскій, General Field-Marshal Prince Baryátinski; Канцлеръ Князь Горчаковъ, Chancellor Prince Gortchakóff, &c. In the same way when addressing persons of these ranks: *Ex.* Ваше

Сіятельство, Your Serene Highness; Егó Превосходи́тельство, His Excellency; Егó Благорóдіе, His Honour; Егó Преосвященство, His Eminence; and the complimentary designations used in writing: Ми́лостивый Госудáрь и Господи́нъ, Dear Sir and Mister, &c. For the sake of politeness, pronouns which relate to the second person are put in capital letters: *Ex.* Я проси́лъ *Васъ* о доставле́ніи мнѣ Ва́шихъ пла́новъ, I asked *you* regarding the furnishing to me of *your* plans.

(14) The initial letters of adjectives relating to God and His Saints: *Ex.* Всевы́шій, Most High; Всеси́льный, Most Mighty; Преподóбный, Reverend; &c.

(15) The initial letters of the designations of governments and tribunals: *Ex* Госудáрственный Совѣ́тъ, State Council; Прави́тельствующій Сенáтъ, Executive Senate; Канцеля́рія Министе́рства Вну́треннихъ Дѣлъ, Chancellory of the Ministry of Home Affairs; &c.

(16) The initial letters of the titles of scientific and educational institutions: *Ex.* Акаде́мія Наýкъ, Academy of Sciences; Минералоги́ческое Общество, Mineralogical Society; Гóрный Институ́тъ, Mining Institute; &c.

*Obs.*—The rules in clauses 11, 12, 15 and 16 are observed in petitions and in business papers generally.

(17) In the initial letters of the titles of books: *Ex.* Путеше́ствіе Вокрýгъ Свѣ́та, Travels Round the World; &c.

(18) In the initial letters of the names of festivals: *Ex.* Свѣ́тлое Воскресе́ніе, Easter Sunday; Благовѣ́щеніе, The Annunciation; Рождество́ Христо́во, Christmas Day, *lit.* Birth of Christ.

(19) In the initial letters of the names of orders: *Ex.* Óрденъ подвя́зки, Order of the Garter; &c.

(20) In the initial letters of the characters in fables, &c.: *Ex.* Одна́жды Лéбедь, Ракъ, и Щýка, &c., Once upon a time a swan, a lobster, and a pike; &c.

## Use of Small Letters.

§ 208. Rules for the use of the letter *a*:—Nouns ending in *о, цо, це,* and *ще,* have, in the nominative and accusative cases of the plural number, *a*: *Ex.* войска́ armies, о́кна windows, стекла́ glasses, ли́ца persons, сердца́ hearts, учи́лища schools, зрѣ́лища spectacles—

*not* войски, окпы, &c. The exception to this rule is я́блоко apple, which makes я́блоки. But all the diminutive nouns ending in ко and це have и, ы: *Ex.* зёрнышко grain, *plur.* зёрнышки, зёркальце mirror, зёркальцы.

§ 209. The letter з in the prepositions воз, из, низ, раз, before the letters к, п, т, х, ц, ч, ш and щ, is changed into с: *Ex.* восклица́ніе exclamation, воспи́танникъ pupil, истреби́ть to destroy, исхо́дъ exodus, исцѣле́ніе cure, нечеза́ть to disappear, происше́ствіе occurrence, исщипа́ть to pinch.

§ 210. The letter i is written before vowels and before the semi-vowel й: *Ex.* прия́тное извѣ́стіе pleasant news, жа́ркій і́юль hot July, &c. Before a consonant the letter *i* is written in the word мíръ universe, and in all words derived therefrom—*Ex.* мiрско́й world, всемíрный universally, Владíміръ Vladímir, &c.—in order to distinguish them from the word миръ, peace, and its derivatives. In foreign words adopted in the Russian language, after the letter ц is written и, and not ы: *Ex.* ци́фра cipher, медици́на medicine, and not цы́фра and медицы́на, although in such instances the pronunciation is the same.

§ 211. Although in the terminations of the diminutive and caressive nouns the form of the letter *е* is preserved, it is pronounced like *и*. Instead, therefore, of writing цвѣто́чикъ blossom, цвѣто́чекъ is written, &c.

§ 212. The double letter *сч* is found at the beginning of the following words only, and their derivatives: сча́стіе prosperity, счётъ account, счастли́вый fortunate, несча́стный unfortunate, разсчётъ calculation, счита́ть to count, &c.

§ 213. Rules for the letter ѣ:—This letter is found at the beginning of two radical words only, viz. ѣхать (ѣздить) to ride or drive, ѣсть to eat. It occurs in the beginning or the middle of the following words and their derivatives:—

А.

Апрѣ́ль, April.

Б.

бесѣ́да, conversation.
бесѣ́дка, summer-house.
блѣ́дный, pale.

болѣ́знь, disease.
брѣ́ю (from бри́ть), I shave.
бѣсъ, demon.
бѣси́ть, to drive mad.
бѣ́шенство, madness.
бѣ́гать, to run.
бѣда́, woe.
бѣ́дный, poor.

бѣдность, poverty.
бѣлый, white.
  бѣльмо, cataract (in the eye).
  бѣлуга, sturgeon.

### В.

встрѣчать, to meet.
вѣдать, to know.
  отвѣдать, to taste.
  вѣдѣніе, knowledge.
  вѣдомость, intelligence.
  вѣдьма, witch.
вѣжливость, politeness.
вѣсть, news.
  исповѣдь, &c., confession.
вѣжди, eyelids.
вѣко, eyelid.
вѣкъ, century.
  вѣчный, eternal.
  вѣчность, eternity.
Вѣна, Vienna.
вѣнецъ, crown.
вѣнокъ, wreath.
вѣникъ, broom.
вѣно, dowry.
вѣра, faith.
  вѣрить, &c., to believe.
вѣсить, to weigh.
  вѣсъ, weight.
  вѣсы, scales.
  вѣшать, to hang.
  повѣсить, ditto.
  завѣса, curtain.
  навѣсъ, verandah.
вѣтвь, branch.
вѣтеръ, wind.
вѣщать, to announce.
  извѣщать, &c., to inform.
  навѣщать, &c., to visit.
вѣха, pole.
вѣять, to blow.
  вѣеръ, fan.

### Г.

Глѣбъ, proper name.
гнѣвъ, anger.
гнѣдой, bay (colour).
гнѣздо, nest.
горѣлки, a game.
грамотѣй, learned man.
грѣхъ, sin.

### Д.

Днѣпръ, Dneiper.
Днѣстръ, Dneister.
доспѣхъ, armour.
дѣва, virgin.
дѣвать, to put.
  одѣвать, to put on.
  издѣваться, &c., to mock.
дѣдъ, grandfather.
дѣйствіе, action.
дѣло, business.
  дѣяніе, act.
дѣлить, to divide.
  опредѣлить, to define.
  раздѣлить, &c., to separate.
дѣти, children.

### Ж.

желѣза, glands.
желѣзо, iron.

### З.

завѣса, curtain.
замѣчаніе, observation.
запавѣсъ, curtain.
заповѣдь, commandment.
застѣнчивость, shyness.
затмѣніе, eclipse.
затѣвать, to project.
звѣзда, star.
звѣрь, wild beast.
змѣй, serpent.
зрѣлый, ripe.
зѣвъ, mouth.
  зѣвать, to yawn.
зѣница, eyeball.

### И

Индѣецъ, Indian.
Индѣйка, turkey.

### К

калѣка, cripple.
клѣть, room.
  клѣтка, cage.
колѣно, knee.
крѣпкій, strong.

### Л

лѣвый, left.
лѣкарь, healer.
   лѣчить, to cure.
(These two words are sometimes spelt with е instead of ѣ, but the latter is more regular.)
   лелѣять, to cuddle.
лѣнь, idleness.
лѣпить, to plaster.
   нелѣпый, absurd.
   великолѣпный, magnificent.
лѣсъ, forest.
   лѣшій, forest imp.
лѣзть, to climb.
   лѣстница, staircase.
лѣто, summer.

### М

медвѣдь, bear (from вѣдать, to know, and мёдъ, honey).
мѣдь, copper.
мѣлъ, chalk.
мѣна, exchange.
   перемѣна, alteration.
   измѣна, &c., treason.
мѣра, measure.
   лицемѣріе, hypocrisy.
   умѣренность, &c., moderation.
мѣсить, to knead.
мѣсто, place.
   вмѣщать, to insert.
   намѣстникъ, viceroy.
мѣсяцъ, month, or moon.
мѣтить, to mark.
   замѣтить, to remark.
   отмѣтить, to make a mark.
мѣхъ, fur.
мѣшать, to mix.
   смѣсь, mixture.
мѣшать, to impede.
   помѣшательство, folly.
   помѣха, &c., obstacle.
мѣшокъ, sack.
мѣщанинъ, burgess.

### Н

надѣяться, to hope.
намѣреніе, intention.
наслѣдство, inheritance.
пасѣкомое, insert.
невѣста, bride.
   невѣстка, daughter-in-law, or sister-in-law.
недѣля, week.
нѣга, indulgence.
нѣдро, womb.
нѣжный, tender.
Нѣманъ, proper name.
нѣмецъ, German.
нѣмой, dumb.
нѣтъ, no, not.

### О

обрѣтать, to find.
   изобрѣтать, to invent.
   пріобрѣтать, to acquire.
обѣдъ, dinner.
обѣдня, mass.
обѣтъ, vow.
обѣщаніе, promise.
орѣхъ, nut.
отвѣтъ, answer.

### П

плѣнъ, captivity.
плѣсень, mildew.
плѣшивый, bald.
побѣда, victory.
повѣтъ, district.
полѣно, log of wood.
понедѣльникъ, Monday.
посѣщать, to visit.
привѣтливость, affability.
примѣръ, example.
прѣсный, sweet (not salt).
пѣгій, piebald.
пѣна, froth.
пѣня, punishment.
пѣнязь, denarius (a coin).
пѣснь, song.
пѣтухъ, cock.
пѣхота, infantry.
пѣшій, pedestrian.
пѣшка, pawn (in chess).

### Р

рѣдкій, rare.

рѣдька, radish.
рѣзать, to cut.
   прорѣха, slit.
рѣзвый, playful.
рѣзной, carved.
рѣка́, river.
рѣпа, turnip.
рѣсни́ца, eyelid.
рѣчь, speech.
   нарѣчіе, dialect.
рѣши́ть, to decide.
рѣшето́, sieve.
   рѣшётка, grating.
рѣять, to pour forth.

### С

свирѣ́ль, reed, pipe.
свирѣпый, ferocious.
свѣжій, fresh.
свѣтъ, light.
   свѣти́ть, to illuminate.
   свѣча́, candle.
   просвѣще́ніе, &c., enlightenment.
слѣдъ, track.
   слѣ́довать, to follow.
   послѣдній, &c., last.
слѣпо́й, blind.
смѣхъ, laughter.
   смѣяться, to laugh.
   смѣшно́й, &c., laughable.
смѣта, estimate.
снѣгъ, snow.
со́вѣсть, conscience.
совѣтъ, advice.
сомнѣ́ніе, doubt.
сосѣдъ, neighbour.
спѣши́ть, to hasten.
стрѣла́, arrow.
стѣна́, wall.
сѣверъ, north.
сѣдло́, saddle.
сѣсть, to sit.
сѣдина́, greyness (of hair).
сѣмя, seed.
сѣни, vestibule.
сѣнь, cover.
   осѣня́ть, to shade.
сѣно, hay.
сѣра, sulphur.

сѣрый, grey.
сѣтовать, to lament.
сѣть, net.
сѣчь, to flog.
сѣять, to sow.

### Т

телѣга, cart.
тѣло, body.
тѣнь, shade.
тѣсный, narrow.
   стѣсня́ть, &c., to crowd.
тѣсто, dough.
тѣшить, to amuse.
   утѣха, amusement.

### У

убѣжда́ть, to convince.
уѣздъ, district.

### Х

хлѣбъ, bread.
хлѣвъ, stye (for animals).
хрѣнъ, horse-radish.

### Ц

цвѣтъ, flower.
   цвѣсти́, to blossom.
цѣвни́ца, flute.
цѣди́ть, to draw off.
цѣли́ть, to heal.
   исцѣля́ть, &c., to cure.
цѣль, mark.
   цѣлить, to aim.
цѣлова́ть, to kiss.
цѣлый, whole.
цѣна́, price.
цѣпь, chain.
цѣпкій, clinging.
   цѣпля́ться, &c., to cling to.
цѣпенѣть, to grow stiff.
цѣпъ, flail.

### Ч

человѣ́къ, man.

Words which have the letter ѣ retain it in all compound and derivative words: *Ex.* вѣра, faith; вѣрую, I believe; вѣрю, I trust; вѣрный, faithful; вѣрность, fidelity; увѣреніе, assurance; увѣренность, confidence; повѣренный, agent; вѣроятіе, probability; достовѣрный, authentic; легковѣрный, credulous; суевѣріе, superstition; &c. Two words only do not follow this rule, viz. надѣяться, to hope, and одѣвать, to dress; from which come надёжда, hope; and одёжда, clothing.

The letter ѣ is written in the syllable нѣ, which is prefixed to pronouns and adverbs: *Ex.* нѣкто, нѣчто, нѣкоторый, нѣсколько, нѣкогда; but the word нéкогда, want of leisure, is written with е.

In the following instances the letter ѣ appears at the end and in the middle of words;—

(1) In the *dative* and *propositional* cases of nouns substantive terminating in *a* and *я*: *Ex.* Слугѣ, to a servant; о судьѣ, about a judge. Excepting those nouns which end in *ія*: *Ex.* Россія, which has Россіи and о Россіи, &c.

(2) In the *prepositional* case of nouns which end in *й*, *ъ* and *ь* of the masculine gender: *Ex.* въ покоѣ, in peace; при столѣ, at a table; въ огнѣ, in the fire. Also in the prepositional case of nouns which end in *o* and *e*: *Ex.* на окнѣ, on the window; въ полѣ, in the field, but those ending in *ie* take *u*; thus, въ имѣніи, in possession; о рѣшéніи, about the decision.

(3) In the *comparative and superlative* degrees which terminate in *ѣe* and *ѣйшій*: *Ex.* свѣтлѣе, свѣтлѣйшій.

(4) In the *numerals* однѣ, двѣ, обѣ, двѣнадцать, двѣсти. In the first and third of these examples the letter ѣ appears in all the cases.

(5) In the *dative* and *prepositional* cases of the pronouns я, ты, себя; thus, мнѣ, тебѣ, о себѣ.

(6) In the *instrumental* case, singular number, of the pronouns кто, что, тотъ, весь; thus, кѣмъ, чѣмъ, тѣмъ, всѣмъ.

(7) In *all the cases* of the plural number of the pronouns тотъ and весь.

(8) In the *nominative* case, plural, of the fem. form of the pronoun of the third person: она́, онѣ́.

(9) In verbs, the first person of the present tense of which ends in ѣю, the letter ѣ occurs in all the tenses and moods, except of брять,

to shave: *Ex.* смѣть, to dare, смѣю, смѣлъ, смѣй. And likewise in all words derived from these verbs: *Ex.* смѣлость, смѣлый, смѣльчакъ, daring, bold, bold fellow, &c.

(10) Except the three verbs, умерѣть to die, терѣть to rub, перѣть to push, and its derivatives, заперѣть to lock, отперѣть to unlock, all have ѣ instead of e before the termination ть of the infinitive mood: *Ex.* смотрѣть, хотѣть, видѣть. These verbs have also ѣ before the terminations лъ of the past tense, indicative mood: *Ex.* смотрѣлъ, хотѣлъ, видѣлъ. The participles and gerunds, and also all words derived from these verbs, likewise maintain the letter ѣ: *Ex.* Видѣвшій, увидѣвъ, видѣніе, привидѣніе, провидѣніе.

(11) In the adverbs вездѣ, внѣ, гдѣ, доколѣ, дотолѣ, здѣсь, кромѣ, нынѣ, отселѣ, подлѣ, вполнѣ, возлѣ, вправѣ, влѣвѣ, вскорѣ, наканунѣ, наединѣ, послѣ. Likewise in nouns adjective formed from these adverbs: *Ex.* внѣшній, здѣшній, нынѣшній, &c.

The letter ѣ also appears before *й* in the terminations of the following nouns—Авдѣй, Алексѣй, Сергѣй, Матѳѣй, грамотѣй, and in the derivatives of the verbs дѣлать and дѣйствовать, such as злодѣй, чародѣй.

§ 214. The letter ѣ is not written in the following cases:—

(1) In the middle of words, after the letters г, к, х, ж, ч, ш, щ, except in the case of the two pronouns кѣмъ and чѣмъ.

(2) When the letter *e* is pronounced like *ё* (*йо* or *o*): *Ex.* лёдъ, мёдъ, шёлъ, плёлъ. Exceptions:—*Substantives*: гнѣзда, звѣзды, сѣдла. *Verbs*: обрѣлъ, and цвѣлъ, and their compounds пріобрѣлъ, изобрѣлъ, расцвѣлъ.

(3) In the designations of races, terminating in *не*: *Ex.* Славяне, Slavs; Россіяне, Russians; Армяне, Armenians; &c.

(4) In foreign words received into the Russian language;— except Апрѣль, April; Вѣна, Vienna; and their derivatives.

> *Obs.*—In order to avoid mistakes in the use of ѣ in words wherein the letter *e* also occurs, it should be observed that ѣ represents the sound on which rests the accent: *Ex.* лелѣять, to fondle; телѣга, cart; сѣверъ, north; Нѣмецъ, German; желѣзо, iron; перемѣна, change; &c.

§ 215. The Greek letter ѳ appears only in the beginning of the following Russian words: ой! этотъ, охъ! ѳкой, ѳтакъ, ѳтакой, and in the beginning and middle of foreign words introduced into the Russian language: *Ex.* ѐхо, октвáторъ, ѳкзáменъ, отáжъ, поэ́ма, поэ́тъ, &c.

§ 216. The letter ѳ, in pronunciation like *ф*, appears in words introduced into Russian from the Greek: (*Ex.* Аѳи́ны Athens, Ѳермопи́лы Thermopylæ, &c.), and also in words taken from the Latin or the French. In such it stands for *th*: *Ex.* Эсѳи́рь Esther, Ѳёдоръ Théodor, Ѳомá Thomas, &c.

§ 217. The letters ъ and ь mark the distinction in the pronunciation of those words ending either in the one or the other. The former gives a hard articulation: *Ex.* столъ table, шестъ pole, матъ mate; but the letter ь gives a soft utterance: *Ex.* столь so much, so many, шесть six, мать mother. The semi-vowels ъ and ь after the sibilant letters ж, ч, ш, щ, mark no kind of distinction in pronunciation: *Ex.* ножъ knife, рожъ rye, мечъ sword, течь to flow, камы́шъ reed, мы́шь mouse. In such cases it must be observed that all nouns of the masculine gender take ъ after the sibilant letters above enumerated: *Ex.* рубе́жъ border, лучъ ray, ключъ key, врачъ doctor, шала́шъ hut, пла́щъ cloak, плю́щъ ivy, &c. The same remark applies to the patronymic nouns: *Ex.* Ива́новичъ, Миха́йловичъ, Петро́вичъ, &c. But nouns of the feminine gender terminate in ь: *Ex.* рожь rye, ночь night, пу́стошь waste ground, по́мощь aid. After the и in the middle of a word, ь is not written: *Ex.* до́чка daughter, то́чка point, stop, пе́чка oven, пти́чка bird, &c.

§ 218. The letter ъ occurs in the genitive case, plural, of nouns ending in *а, о*, and *ще*: *Ex.* слугá слугъ, окно́ око́нъ, учи́лище учи́лищъ; likewise in the same case and number of the following words:—ты́сяча ты́сячъ, са́жень са́женъ; and in certain cases, singular and plural, of the masculine and neuter forms of the pronouns нашъ and вашъ.

§ 219. The letter ь occurs—

(1) In the infinitive mood of active and neuter verbs: *Ex.* смотрѣ́ть, бѣ́гать. Likewise before the suffix *ся* in reflective, reciprocal, and common verbs: *Ex.* хвали́ться, сража́ться, надѣ́яться.

(2) (*a*) In the 2nd person singular of the present and future tenses, indicative mood, of active and neuter verbs: *Ex.* ви́дишь, побѣ́гаешь;—(*b*) in the 1st and 2nd person singular, and 2nd person

plural, of the present and future tenses of reflective, reciprocal, and common verbs: *Ex.* хвалю́сь, хва́лишься, хва́литесь, &c.

(3) In the 2nd person of both numbers of the imperative mood: *Ex.* оста́вь, оста́вьте, &c. Exception: perfect aspect of the verb ложи́ться, лягъ, which in the 2nd person plural of the imperative mood makes лягте.

(4) Words taken from foreign languages, after the letter л have ь: *Ex.* А́льпы the Alps, а́льтъ (musical term *alto*), брилья́нтъ brilliant, &c.

### Proper Use of Separate Words.

§ 220. The negative adverb *не* is written separately—

(1) Before possessive and circumstantial adjectives: *Ex.* *не* ру́сскій, *не* золото́й, *не* зде́шній, *не* вчера́шній, &c.

(2) Before numerals: *Ex. не* оди́нъ, *не* впервы́й, &c.

(3) Before the pronouns: *Ex. не* онъ, *не* нашъ, *не* тотъ, &c.

(4) Before verbs and adverbs: *Ex. не* ви́жу, *не* жела́лъ, *не* ви́дя, *не* жела́я, &c.

§ 221. The negative adverb *не* is written conjointly—

(1) With nouns adjective, and adverbs of quality: *Ex.* *не*бога́тый poor, *не*весёлый sad, *не*бога́то poorly, *не*ве́село sadly.

> *Obs.*—If adverse conjunctions precede adjectives or adverbs of quality, the negative adverb *не* is written separately: *Ex. не* бога́тый но сы́тный обѣдъ, *not* a rich, but a copious dinner; оно́ хотя́ *не* ве́село но поле́зно, although (it is) *not* cheerful, yet (it is) useful.

(2) With participles: *Ex. не*зави́сящій *in*dependent, *не*дви́жимый *im*moveable, &c.

(3) The negative adverb *не* is written conjointly with words which either have no signification of their own, as *не*дугъ sickness, *не*людимъ misanthrope, *не*чести́вый impious, *не*́навнсть hatred, *не*па́стье bad weather;—or else an altogether different meaning, as *не*изрѣче́нный unutterable, *не*пра́вда untruth, it is not true, *не*прія́тель enemy, *не*поко́рностъ disobedience.

§ 222. The particle *ни* is written conjointly only with the following words: никто́, никако́й, нигдѣ́, никуда́, ника́къ, никогда́. In all other instances it is written separately: *Ex.* ни ско́лько, ни ма́ло: онъ не умѣ́етъ *ни* чита́ть *ни* писа́ть, he can neither read nor write.

§ 223. When the prepositions за, по, на, изъ, съ, въ are joined with other parts of speech, and thus form adverbs or conjunctions, they are written conjointly with the word to which they are joined: *Ex.* зачѣмъ, затѣмъ, потому́, поутру́, напримѣръ, наканунѣ, the day before; и́встари, of old; сначала, снизу, сверху, винзу́, сверху́, справо, спрочемъ, наконецъ, &c. But if these prepositions do not form adverbs or conjunctions, and govern some one case or another, then they are written separately: *Ex.* За тѣмъ са́домъ нашъ домъ, Our house (is) behind that garden; Пойду́ по тому берегу, I will go along that bank; Смотри на примѣръ добрыхъ товарищей, Look to the example of good companions; Онъ уѣхалъ со всѣмъ своимъ семействомъ, He went away with his whole family; &c.

§ 224. The conditional conjunction, бы (бъ) is only joined in the two following instances: чтобы, дабы́. In all others it is written separately: *Ex.* Я пришёлъ бы къ вамъ, если бы имѣлъ время, I would have come to you if I had had time.

§ 225. The copulative conjunction же (жъ) before various parts of speech is written separately: *Ex.* тотъ же, однако же, что жъ, иди жé, смотри же. It is also written separately in the comparative conjunction такъ же: *Ex.* Ри́мляне были такъ же славны, какъ и греки, The Romans were as famous as the Greeks. But in the case of the copulative conjunction также it is not separated: *Ex.* Я также былъ въ Петергофѣ, I was also at Peterhoff. The word то́же, when it implies uniformity, is written conjointly: *Ex.* Я то́же пое́ду, I likewise will go. But when it is used as a pronoun it is written separately: *Ex.* Онъ то же отвѣча́лъ мнѣ что и вамъ, He answered me the same as he did you.

## Copulatives.

§ 226. A hyphen is called a *copulative* (знакъ соединительный), and it may serve to connect two or more separate words: *Ex.* Генералъ-адъюта́нтъ, General Aide-de-camp; физико-математическій, physico-mathematical.

§ 227. Copulatives may connect—

(1) Two nouns substantive: *Ex.* Генералъ-фельдмаршалъ, штабъ-офицеръ, General Field-Marshal, superior officer, &c.

(2) Two adjectives: *Ex.* Сѣверо-Американскіе Штаты, North-American States. Likewise adjectives with substantives: *Ex.* Нижне-Камчатскъ, Lower Kamtchatsa, &c.

(3) Numerals with adjectives: *Ex.* трёхъ-угóльный, triangular, &c.

(4) Prepositions with various parts of speech, *i. e.* when such a union forms an adverb: по-рýсски, in Russian; по-брáтски, after the manner of brothers; по-мóему, in my way; во-вторы́хъ, secondly, &c.

(5) Compound prepositions, such as изъ-за, изъ-подъ, &c.

(6) The conjunctions то, либо, with various parts of speech: *Ex.* кто-то, какóй-то, гдѣ-то, кто-лúбо, когдá-лúбо.

§ 228. Copulatives, or hyphens, serve also to connect words which are disjointed by being carried on from one line to another, and of this mention is made below.

## Disjointing of Words.

§ 229. In carrying on words from one line to another, the following rules should be observed:—

(1) To carry on regular syllables: *Ex.* бла-го-ра-зýм-ный че-ло-вѣкъ, discreet man.

(2) In compound words, or those made up with other parts of speech, to disjoint their component parts: *Ex.* Цáрь-грáдъ, Нов-гóродъ, вос-хóдъ, море-хóдъ, отъ-ѣздъ, &c.

(3) Words of one syllable cannot be carried on from one line to another: *Ex.* гро-мъ (громъ), стра-сть (страсть), вол-къ (волкъ), цар-ствъ (царствъ).

(4) One letter only of polysyllabic words cannot be transferred to another line: *Ex.* армí-я, лилí-ю.

## Contraction of Words.

§ 230. Contracted words must end ordinarily in a consonant: *Ex.* имя прил. (прилагáтельное), муж. род., множ. числ., дат. пад.

§ 231. The following comprise the more commonly used contractions:—г. (господúнъ), г-жа (госпожá), м. г. (мúлостивый госудáрь), напр. (напримѣръ), т. е. (то есть), и проч. (и прóчее), п. т. д. (и такъ далѣе), и. т. п. (и томý подóбное), с. п. б. (Санктпетербýргъ), по Р. Х. (по Рождествѣ Христóвомъ), отъ С. М. (отъ Сотворéнія Мíра), вм. (вмѣсто).

THE END.

www.ingramcontent.com/pod-product-compliance
Lightning Source LLC
Chambersburg PA
CBHW030358170426
43202CB00010B/1418